Battle Cry

✝

GOOD vs. dEVIL

Bruce Dillender

ISBN 978-1-64458-669-3 (paperback)
ISBN 978-1-64458-670-9 (digital)

Christian Faith Publishing, Inc.
832 Park Avenue
Meadville, PA 16335
www.christianfaithpublishing.com

Author Photograph courtesy of Jen Dillender Photography

Scripture quotations are taken from the Holy Bible, New Living Translation, copyright ©1996, 2004, 2007, 2013, 2015 by Tyndale House Foundation. Used by permission of Tyndale House Publishers, Inc., Carol Stream, Illinois 60188. All rights reserved.

Printed in the United States of America

Contents

Acknowledgments

Battle Cry is dedicated to my wife of forty-two years, Karen. Although we've been through our fair share of darkness, hand in hand, we never stopped walking toward the Light. For her faithfulness, Karen is the most caring and giving person I know. Thanks to her passion for helping those in need, seven years ago, we started a homeless outreach ministry, RV Ambassadors for Christ. For my faithfulness, I was prompted by the Spirit to write *Battle Cry*. For over four years, I would wake up at all hours of the night, wide-eyed and spiritually inspired, spending countless hours researching scripture, writing, and editing. Through it all, I want to thank Karen for her support and encouragement.

I thank Lucille Foster and Mary Jo Lyons for their support, encouragement, and editorial suggestions throughout the writing process. I thank my son, Joshua (J. D.) for his real-life example of how to have a personal relationship with Christ, and how to follow the prompting of the Spirit to further the Kingdom of God. I want to thank the youth outreach ministry Young Life, for following the example of Christ, by literally going where young people are, on their turf and in their culture, building bridges of authentic friendship. Both our homeless outreach ministry and my counseling ministry are modeled after Christ's example of going where people are.

Above all, I thank God the Father, for His unconditional love, and the opportunity to be in a personal relationship with Him. I thank God the Son, Jesus Christ, for the pain and suffering He endured. I thank God, the Holy Spirit, for the strength, the guidance, and courage, to write *Battle Cry*. To God, I give all the glory!

Introduction

When it comes to God and spirituality, we all have our personal opinions and beliefs. If you don't believe in God, would you at least agree, there has to be more to life than what meets the eye? If so, why not explore the possibility of God? What do you have to lose? What might you gain? If you already believe in God, open your heart and mind because there is so much more to discover and learn about the mystery of God and spirituality.

God is, and always has been, a loving God of relationship. Although God's Word reveals His love for us, His action speaks louder. Because we couldn't save ourselves, He took action by sending His one and only Son to die for us and save us. Because we are weak in Spirit and predisposed to follow our sinful nature, He took action by sending the Holy Spirit to provide spiritual strength and guidance. Because He wants us to know and feel His love, He continues to take action by pursuing a personal relationship with us. Matthew 9:10–13 says, "Later, Matthew invited Jesus and his disciples to his home as dinner guests, along with many tax collectors and other disreputable sinners. But when the Pharisees saw this, they asked his disciples, 'Why does your teacher eat with such scum?' When Jesus heard this, he said, 'healthy people don't need a doctor—sick people do.' Then he added, 'Now go and learn the meaning of this Scripture: I want you to show mercy, not offer sacrifices. For I have come to call not those who think they are righteous, but those who know they are sinners.'"

When Jesus says "sick people need a doctor," He is referring to spiritual sickness. Spiritual sickness manifests itself in sin. Since we all sin, we are all spiritually sick. Does the thought of you being spiritually sick bother you? Do you think you are righteous, or do you know you are a sinner? If you know you are a sinner, Jesus came to specifically call you. Jesus uses metaphors throughout the Bible to help us understand His teachings. In this one, He uses something we understand, physical sickness, to teach us about something we don't understand, spiritual sickness. When physically sick, we pursue a medical doctor to heal us. With little or no hesitation, we have the faith to trust the diagnosis and treatment. Because we are spiritually sick, we need to pursue a spiritual doctor, and His name is Jesus Christ. Without hesitation, we need to have the faith to trust His diagnosis and treatment. We are all spiritually sick and the treatment is a loving relationship with Him.

We all struggle with sin in our lives, but it appears we are reaching new lows. We continue to shun God, and it's becoming more obvious, we couldn't care less about what He thinks or feels. We've allowed the efforts of some to become the reality of many. We've lost prayer in school, and we're slowly losing Christ in Christmas. There's even talk about removing "In God We Trust" from our currency. We're evolving into something more difficult to recognize as "Godly." It's become a common occurrence for many in positions of authority to be accused of unscrupulous behavior. Even something as precious as freedom, has become more about self and less about God and country. Hate and violence have become the common response to the major issues facing society today.

When we consider how often we are shocked, disgusted, sickened, and horrified by another mass shooting, we can no longer deny the existence of evil. Even law enforcement representatives, and the media, refer to these horrific acts as "acts of pure evil." Although God is seldom mentioned or discussed, it seems most would agree, evil does exist. We must stop ignoring the obvious signs. We have a problem, and it's spiritual. When someone's behavior indicates they are struggling with a conflict within, family members, friends, or schoolmates, must either make the effort to help this person, or take the necessary action to report their behavior to someone who can. We must not continue to allow someone to cross over the line between what's right and wrong, good and evil.

Battle Cry offers thought provoking insight into God and spirituality, but the importance of reading and studying the Bible cannot be overstated. But here's the problem. When we read and study the Bible, we can find ourselves getting confused or overwhelmed. Then, when we try to gain insight from others, because of all the personal opinions and beliefs, we get even more confused. Although the Bible is the obvious place to get answers, *Battle Cry* could be exactly what you need, at precisely the right time. When it comes to God and His plans, nothing is by chance. So by virtue of the fact you are in possession of this book, you are one of the countless reasons why it was written.

The mission of *Battle Cry* is to shine the Light into the darkness, to increase knowledge and awareness of God and spirituality, and to gain a better understanding of the spiritual battles that occur within us. Satan is fully aware that by reading *Battle Cry* and referencing the Bible, you will gain insight into the power struggle that exists between good and evil. If you have random thoughts influencing you to stop reading, don't stop reading. Rely on the strength of the Spirit to get you through. Your dependence on God is your only hope of defeating Satan, whose "soul" purpose is to keep you separated from God.

1
Spirituality

To understand spirituality and what it means to be spiritual, we must be able and willing to acknowledge the influence of the unseen spiritual world and its effects on the seen world. Although God and Satan are both a part of this same unseen spiritual world, we have little hesitation to acknowledge the influence of God, but have difficulty acknowledging the influence of Satan. If you believe in one, you must believe in the other.

When we think about God, we usually envision Jesus Christ. This causes us to equate the size of God with the size of Jesus. When we apply this same logic to Satan, we envision this character with a pitch fork and pointed tail. This couldn't be further from the Truth. The size and complexity of God, Satan, and the spiritual realm, is beyond what we can comprehend or imagine. Genesis 1:1–2 says, "In the beginning God created the heavens and the earth. The earth was formless and empty, and darkness covered the deep waters. And the Spirit of God was hovering over the surface of the waters." God is so massive, He created the heavens and the Earth, He hovered over the surface of the waters, and He can live in every one of us at the same time. The spiritual massiveness of God should put the spiritual size of Satan into perspective.

There are unseen spiritual forces constantly vying for our attention to influence us. The Spirit of God wants us to listen and respond to nothing but the good and positive spiritual influences. Satan wants us to listen and respond to nothing but the bad and negative spiritual influences. How we respond to these influences has a negative and positive impact on our personal lives. It determines how good or bad we are. It affects our earthly relationships and our relationship with God. Our awareness and acknowledgment of these unseen forces, and their influence on our lives, is at the very core of our spirituality. It's what enables us to feel raw emotion. It's that gut feeling that gives us pause before a bad decision is made. It's the guilty conscience after. It's the ability to know there's something going on we feel, but don't always understand. This spiritual feeling and emotion is what sets us apart from all other created beings. It's what gives us the ability to be in a relationship with a living and loving God, like no other part of creation.

We can tap into our spirituality and become more spiritual by acknowledging the Spirit in us. The Spirit enables us to recognize God in all creation, starting with our miraculously created bodies. Study the design of the eye enabling us to see all the wonders of the world in living color. Examine the design and strength of our bone structure enabling us to stand upright. From the ribcage protecting our vital organs, to the skull protecting our brain, God's design is specific. Observe the complex network of blood flow throughout our body, from the smallest veins, to our amazing beating heart. Marvel at the complex functionality of the brain, from its ability to instantly think, to its capacity to store and retrieve information. Now tap into your raw emotion and your ability to feel and know love.

We have two choices; we can deny or embrace the Spirit. By denying the Spirit, we will remain spiritually dormant. By embracing the Spirit, we begin a spiritual awakening, and our body becomes the temple of the Holy Spirit. First Corinthians 6:19–20 says, "Don't you realize that your body is the temple of the Holy Spirit, who lives in you and was given to you by God? You do not belong to yourself, for God bought you with a high price. So you must honor God with your body." Do we consider and treat our bodies as a temple, a shrine, a sanctuary, a holy place? Do we give any thought at all to the high price Christ paid by physically dying on the cross? Instead, don't we just take our bodies for granted?

As we continue to acknowledge and recognize God in all creation, we must also look at the external intricacies of creation. Look at the miraculously created sky, trees, lakes, rivers, oceans, and mountains. Look at our planet and how it exists in the solar system with the sun, moon, and the entire universe. Our ability to acknowledge God in all creation is dependent on our ability to acknowledge the Holy Spirit. If you look around at all you see, hear, touch, and feel, and you're not able to recognize or acknowledge God in anything, then you're in need of a spiritual awakening. You need the influence of the Spirit to help you set aside the noise and distractions from the brain. You need the guidance of the Spirit to help you decipher what you truly think and feel. The Spirit will help you acknowledge God in everything, so your heart can be touched by the Truth. If you continue to deny God in everything, you will remain spiritually dormant and undeveloped. You could find yourself literally dying without God. Physical death without God is spiritual life eternal without Him.

Spirituality is about recognizing the unseen spiritual forces at work attempting to influence our decisions and direction in life. Where there is potential for Light, there is potential for dark. Where there is potential for Good, there is potential for evil. Where there is potential for plea-sure, there is potential for pain. It all comes down to the personal choices we make. Every personal choice affects our reality and what we experience. It's also important to understand, our spirituality not only affects our reality and life in the flesh, but it also affects our spiritual life eternal. That's right, spiritual life eternal, never-ending.

Life usually becomes more difficult because of the ungodly choices we make. For that, we have only ourselves to blame. Yet we are so quick to blame and cuss God when nothing seems to be going our way, or the way we think it should. Are we as quick to praise and thank God when everything seems to be going our way, or the way we think it should? Our response to the ups and downs of life is a reflection of our spiritual condition. Even when things don't seem to be going well, if we are strong in Spirit, we can still see the positive and good in our life. Paul tells us in Philippians 4:11–13, "Not that I was ever in need, for I have learned to be content with whatever I have. I know how to live on almost nothing or with everything. I have learned the secret of living in every situation, whether it is with a full stomach or empty, with plenty or little. For I can do everything through Christ, who gives me strength." Paul reveals the secret of being content no matter the circumstances. It's finding our strength in Christ.

No matter how spiritually developed we become, we do not have the intellectual ability to understand everything spiritual, and everything God. If we are influenced into thinking we have developed such a level of understanding, this thinking would never come from the Spirit of Truth. This is important to understand because as we share the love of God, we must remain humble. It's what attracts those interested in God to pause and listen. Jesus says in Matthew 5:14–16, "You are the light of the world—like a city on a hilltop that cannot be hidden. No one lights a lamp and then puts it under a basket. Instead, a lamp is placed on a stand, where it gives light to everyone in the house. In the same way, let your good deeds shine out for all to see, so that everyone will praise your heavenly Father."

Our Light shines by what we say, but it shines brightest by what we do. When the opportunity becomes available, we must be willing to share Christ in a heartfelt and personal way. Although everyone is not as gifted in sharing the Gospel as a preacher might be, God still expects us to witness for Christ. Witnessing in the workplace, or while hanging out with friends is important, yet most fail to make the effort. When the opportunity to witness becomes apparent and fear rears its ugly head, Satan will use that fear to cause us to miss the opportunity. We become a tool of Satan, instead of an instrument of God. God wants us to use every opportunity to be a witness for Christ and further the Kingdom of God. Jesus says in Matthew 10:32–33, "Everyone who acknowledges me publicly here on earth, I will also acknowledge before my Father in heaven. But everyone who denies me here on earth, I will also deny before my Father in heaven." Think about this the next time you allow your fear to cause you to miss an opportunity to witness for Christ.

The most common questions I get when discussing spirituality is, "How do you feel the Spirit?" or "How do you hear God?" Then, there's usually a follow-up statement of, "I've never felt anything spiritual." or "I've never heard God." What effort are you personally making to feel or hear God? Are you waiting for this miraculous experience to unfold where the Holy Spirit comes swooping down to engulf your innermost being? If the process was that easy, everyone would feel the Spirit, everyone would hear God, everyone would be a follower of Christ, and everyone would be saved. Our spiritual development and spiritual condition is influenced by every personal choice we make. It requires a constant and exerted effort on our part. The more spiritually developed we become, the more likely we will feel or hear God. So again, what effort are you personally making to feel or hear God?

Our spirituality is specifically tied to our faith in Jesus Christ. God in the flesh, sent here to literally be seen, heard, and experienced, was our chance to comprehend who He truly is. By His teachings, His response to questions, His miracles, His sacrifice on the cross, and His ability to conquer the grave; God's power, God's wisdom, and God's grace, were on display for all to see. Specific to God's plan, Christ was born of a virgin, pure from the beginning, without sin to the day He died in the flesh. This physical display of a pure and sinless God crucified on the cross, brings understanding to the Truth of God's unconditional love.

When we accept Christ as our personal Savior, we begin a personal relationship with a living, loving, and almighty God. If you're making little or no effort in the relationship, how would you expect the relationship to grow? Is this the way you approach your earthly relationships? Relationships are a two-way street. No relationship can flourish without an effort from both participants. Fortunately, God has fully and completely done His part. It's up to each of us to do ours. Our part is to first choose Christ. Then, we must make the personal effort to spend time with Him and His Word. We can then experience how the Spirit will move in each of us. So if you don't feel the Spirit, if you don't feel His Love, who is failing to make the effort, God or you? Don't you think He's done enough?

If you have the habit of comparing your walk with Christ to what you think others are experiencing, stop doing that. Everybody's walk is uniquely different. We all find God at different times, different ages, and different circumstances. Some find God when they are children, others as teenagers, and some as adults. Sadly, some never find God at all. It's not as important when you find God. What's most important is that you do eventually find Him. Once you find God, you must embrace the opportunity to get to know Him better. Spend time talking with Him.

Spend time just being with Him. If you're not talking and spending time with Him, how in the world would you expect to hear or feel Him? The most important aspect of communication in any relationship is listening. Don't miss the opportunity to be still and silent when spending time with God. This is often the best opportunity to hear and feel Him.

The *Bible*, the Word of God, is the key to unlocking the mystery of spirituality through faith. We must be willing to use this God-given key. If you have a Bible, make the effort to open it and discover what God wants you to know. If you don't have a Bible, find one you can understand and relate to, one that spiritually motivates you. The *Bible* provides the knowledge we need to help us through this very confusing and calamity filled existence. It provides insight and answers to life's questions by providing stories and parables to help us make better sense out of the godly principles we need to live by. It makes God's presence throughout time known by documenting actual events. Some writers heard God's voice. Some witnessed His miracles. Some were God's chosen prophets and received His Word through the Spirit. Can you believe that some writers actually walked with Christ? The Bible has survived the test of time, because the Word of God is the Truth. The fact that it's available today is a miracle. It is a testament to how critically important it is for us to spend time becoming more familiar with its teachings. What a shame to let such a precious gift go to waste.

To develop spiritually, we must devote the time to gain the knowledge available in God's Word. As we gain the knowledge, we can better understand the all-knowing and all-powerful God. We become more aware of the power and the presence of the Holy Spirit. As we grow in Spirit, we will increase faith. Our faith will help improve our personal relationship with Christ. It will grow into a stronger and more mature relationship, one built on trust. By trusting God, we will understand our need to depend on Christ. John 14:6 says, "I am the way, the truth, and the life. No one can come to the Father except through me."

Spirituality is an ongoing, life-changing transformation. We must transform from less of who we are to more of who God wants us to be. Paul says in Ephesians 4:22–23, "Throw off your old sinful nature and your former way of life, which is corrupted by lust and deception. Instead, let the Spirit renew your thoughts and attitudes." Paul is teaching us, the Spirit has the ability to actively renew our thoughts and attitude, inspiring us to make more good choices. It will give us the courage to make fewer bad choices, influenced by our own personal desires, and the desires of Satan.

As we become more aware of what the Spirit is doing within us, we will develop a more confident, meaningful, and loving relationship with Christ. But unfortunately, there's Good News and bad news. The Good News is, living in the Spirit and walking with Christ in a loving relationship, will stimulate spiritual growth and bring much joy to our heart. The bad news is there's a negative spiritual force also vying for our attention. It's dark, it's ugly, it's aggressive, and it's relentless. It tries to separate and alienate us from Christ, which brings much sadness to our heart. It has the ability to negatively impact our reality. This negative spiritual force is the evil and dark side of spirituality and Satan is directly involved with every aspect of it. The Bible refers to it as warfare; we also know it as spiritual warfare.

2

Spiritual Warfare

Spiritual warfare dates back to a fallen angel named Lucifer. This fallen angel, better known to us as Satan or the devil, rebelled against God. His rebellion continued in the garden, as he successfully influenced Eve to sin, and it continues today in his attempts to influence us to sin. If you're having trouble wrapping your brain around Satan being here today, he's got you right where he wants you. By not believing the d*evil* and *evil* exists, when he spiritually attacks, you won't be aware, and you certainly won't be prepared to defend yourself. This makes you completely vulnerable. As you witness what's going on in the world today, can you deny the evidence supporting the existence of evil?

To understand spirituality and how it relates to spiritual warfare, we must look back at the beginning. In Genesis 1:26 God said, "Let us make human beings in our image, to be like us." The use of *our* image, and to be like *us*, refers to the plurality of God known as the Trinity. The Trinity that was present during creation exists today in the Father, the Son, and the Holy Spirit. Each had very distinct roles in creation, and each has very distinct roles in our spiritual life today. In John 17:5 Jesus says, "Now

Father, bring me into the glory we shared before the world began." This confirms the Son of God existed before the world began, before creation as we know it. In John 17:24, Jesus again refers to His existence before the world began by saying, "Father, I want these whom you have given me to be with me where I am. Then they can see all the glory you gave me because you loved me even before the world began!" From a human perspective, it's impossible for us to fathom the size and complexity of the spiritual realm. Our understanding of spirituality is often based on what we can see or imagine. But there is so much more to spirituality we can't see, and it's beyond what we can imagine.

God warned Adam about the knowledge of good and evil. Genesis 2:16–17 says, "But the Lord God warned him, 'You may freely eat the fruit of every tree in the garden—except the tree of the knowledge of good and evil. If you eat its fruit, you are sure to die.'" Genesis 2:18 says, "Then the Lord God said, 'It is not good for the man to be alone. I will make a helper who is just right for him.'" Adam and Eve enjoyed a close and personal relationship with God until Satan influenced Eve to eat of the forbidden fruit. Eve gave some to Adam, and he also ate. Genesis 3:22 says, "Then the Lord God said, 'Look, the human beings have become like us, knowing both good and evil. What if they reach out, take fruit from the tree of life, and eat it? Then they will live forever!'" It appears we were created to live in the presence of God, without knowing good and evil, absent of sin, decay, and suffering. But because we gained the knowledge of good and evil, we lost paradise. Genesis 3:23 says, "So the Lord God banished them from the Garden of Eden, and he sent Adam out to cultivate the ground from which he had been made."

Over time, our disobedience and sinful behavior got incessantly worse. Genesis 6:1–3 says, "Then the people began to multiply on the earth, and daughters were born to them. The Sons of God saw the beautiful women and took any they wanted as their wives. Then the LORD said, 'My Spirit will not put up with humans for such a long time, for they are only mortal flesh. In the future, their normal lifespan will be no more than 120 years.'" Satan has been successfully influencing our behavior, and negatively affecting our lives, since the beginning. We went from living in a garden, created to live without knowing evil, to a lifespan of no more than 120 years, knowing evil. God was obviously not pleased. His disappointment is felt by the fact His Spirit would not tolerate what we had become, so therefore, He limited our normal lifespan. Do you think He's anymore pleased with us today?

Our biblical history reveals, since the very beginning, we have been vulnerable to the influence of Satan. We continue to be vulnerable because our sinful nature and our attraction to the darkness of evil, makes us easy targets of the devil. To become less vulnerable to his attacks, we must become more enlightened and turn our backs on the darkness. We need to turn our face toward God, and walk toward the Light. If we're not walking toward God, we're either standing still, or walking away from Him. Revelation 3:15–16 says, "I know all things you do, that you are neither hot nor cold. I wish you were one or the other! But since you are like lukewarm water, neither hot nor cold, I will spit you out of my mouth!" God is telling us, we must pursue Him with all our heart.

The amount of time we dedicate to pursing God confirms our true heart. When we fail to dedicate time to pursue God, we are in essence turning our back on Him. When we turn our back on God, we don't need much influence from Satan to make ungodly choices. Satan just watches and waits, and usually, we do enough to ourselves without much spiritual attack. But as soon as we make the personal effort to pursue God and start walking toward Him, the devil takes action and spiritually attacks. He wants to influence us to turn back toward the darkness. It's similar to a game of Chess. It's strategic and dependent upon the previous move. But unlike the game of Chess, the stakes couldn't be higher. It's literally a game of spiritual Light and darkness, both in this life, and life eternal.

Spiritual warfare is also like a boxing match, so we must take an active role to defend ourselves. If we don't spiritually defend ourselves, we can't possibly win battles that are spiritual. We will continue to be influenced to do things that are not pleasing to God. Eventually, we feel completely defeated, helpless, hopeless, and depressed. To combat this, we must train, wear the armor of God, and counter punch. Otherwise, we'll just stand there and get a beat down. This is exactly what's happening in the world today, we're getting a beat down.

By not believing or ignoring the unseen spiritual forces at work against us, we won't recognize, acknowledge, or understand their impact on us. We will fail to prepare and will surely lose in spiritual battle. Our defeat will result in more sinful choices and destructive behavior. It will lead to a life of spiritual tragedy. By believing and becoming more aware of the unseen spiritual forces at work against us, we will recognize, acknowledge, and understand their impact on us. We will prepare and take an active role in defending ourselves. We will win more spiritual battles, resulting in less sinful choices and destructive behavior. It will lead to a life of spiritual joy. We can live a life dependent upon the Spirit of God. We can begin to live a spiritual life of optimism, positivity, and hope. We will be more consistent in making choices pleasing to God. Eventually we will rise above the darkness, to live life abundant, full of joy and blessings as God intended. Which are you choosing, a life of spiritual tragedy, or a life of spiritual joy? After all, it is a choice.

For more evidence of an attacking devil, please take time to read Matthew 4:1–11 and Luke 4:1–13. These verses are about Satan having the audacity to tempt Jesus, the Son of God. This exposes a very determined and aggressive enemy. Think about it, knowing Jesus was the Son of God, why would Satan believe he would have any chance of influencing Him with his lies? Why would Satan think he would have any chance at influencing Christ to sin? Was it because Christ was in the flesh? Christ, God in the flesh, was not vulnerable, and although there was no chance to influence Him, it didn't stop Satan from trying. It's important to note that Satan used Scripture in his attempt to influence Jesus. It's even more important to note that Jesus used scripture to defend Himself. It teaches us, we can't win spiritual battles with our own words and strength. We must depend on the Word of God, the strength of the Spirit, and the name of Jesus Christ to win spiritual battles. This explains why the Word of God is identified as the sword in the list of weapons to be used against Satan in spiritual battle. Christ, by example, showed us how to take up the sword of Truth to defend ourselves and defeat Satan in spiritual battle.

So if Satan was there in the beginning to tempt Eve, and he was there to tempt Jesus, why would we have any doubt, he is here doing the same thing to us? The Truth is, the devil is here, he will not leave us alone, and we are naturally drawn to evil. In John 8:44 Jesus says, "For you are the children of your father the devil, and you love to do the evil things he does. He was a murderer from the beginning. He has always hated the truth, because there is no truth in him. When he lies, it is consistent with his character; for he is a liar and the father of lies." First Peter 5:8–9 says, "Stay alert! Watch out for your great enemy, the devil. He prowls around like a roaring lion, looking for someone to devour. Stand firm against him, and be strong in your faith. Remember that your family of believers all over the world is going through the same kind of suffering you are." He's the enemy. He wants to devour. He's spiritually attacking our family of believers all over the world. Doesn't this shed Light on why there's so much darkness and suffering?

We are able to experience and engage in spiritual warfare because of the Holy Spirit. The Spirit helps us to recognize, that there's more to life than what we see and experience in the flesh. He helps us to understand, the only way to successfully win in spiritual battle is to depend on God, and rely on His strength, not ours. As we win spiritual battles, we will grow closer in our relationship with Christ. The closer our relationship with God, the more faith we'll have. After all, when it comes to God, it all comes down to faith. If we lack faith, we will lack the trust necessary to depend on God's strength. We will depend on our own strength, and we will lose spiritual battles. When we lose spiritual battles we encounter personal failure, usually associated with ungodly choices resulting in sinful behavior. Some of our failures will drop us to our knees, which by the way, is a great place to pray for God's grace, mercy, and forgiveness. When we do fail, we should never lose hope, because God will use our failure as an opportunity to move our heart. No matter where we are in our struggles, as soon as we make the decision to trust God, He will provide the strength we need to rise above our circumstances.

We need to embrace spiritual warfare from the perspective of being both human and spiritual. Although we are flesh and blood human, we have the presence of the Holy Spirit. We have input from the brain, mixed with the emotion of the heart, inspired by the Spirit. This is where spiritual warfare takes place. Where both the Spirit of God and Satan are attempting to influence the decisions we make and the action we take. The action we ultimately take not only impacts the moment, but it can have a profound impact on our future. Some decisions and action can instantly and dramatically change our lives. There will always be benefits and consequences to every choice we make. Although the spiritual realm can influence us, we are ultimately responsible for our actions. We are personally responsible to maintain control of our destiny. The devil can't make us do anything, we allow him to influence us.

You are like the captain of your own ship. Your hands are on the wheel. You control your course and destiny. Unless you hand over the control, no one can take control and steer your vessel. When your ship is affected by Satan's strong winds and raging seas, to keep you out of harm's way, you can change your course. Don't you love how God created us to be completely independent vessels? We have the ability to function independently without any other power source. By simply resting or sleeping, we are somehow naturally energized. The food we consume enables us to refuel ourselves and create more energy. We independently process food and excrete waste. Our vessels are capable of functioning and surviving in excess of a hundred years. It's hard to believe our vessels, our created bodies, are so incredibly made. Knowing this, shouldn't we take better care of our vessels?

Thanks to the brain function and the physical ability God gave us, the environment in which we have the responsibility to operate our independent vessels has drastically improved. Most have evolved from an existence of survival, to one of comfort. We hunted food for survival; now we buy food from a store. We found shelter by living in caves, now we live in dwellings built with strong materials. We kept warm and cooked food on an open fire, now we have heaters to keep warm, and stoves for cooking. We struggled to find fresh water, now with the turn of a handle, or the twist of a cap, most have safe drinking water. We preserved food by keeping it in a box with ice, hence the name ice box. Now we preserve food by keeping it in a refrigerator. We lit fires, candles, and lanterns for light, now we have electrical grids, and with the flick of a switch, *let there be light.*

Do you thank God for the comforts you enjoy? Or do you take these comforts for granted? We could never have imagined how television, cell phones, the internet, and social media, would become such a useful resource for communicating, gaining knowledge, and entertainment. Although these blessings can be of benefit, they can also be a major distraction. Anything that distracts us from what's most important, our personal relationship with Christ, is idolatry. Idolatry is a sin, and obviously not spiritually healthy. In spiritual warfare, Satan uses this technology as a weapon. If you wonder if this is true, we need to be reminded of a time when there was less technology. A time when we were more focused on our personal lives, the lives of our family, and the lives of those in our community. We were a people and a nation with our top priorities being God, family, and country. In today's world, with so many distractions vying for our attention, we have become less focused on God, and our priorities have changed. They have become less about God's ways and more about our ways, and the ways of the world.

In spiritual warfare, Satan will use our personal religious beliefs to spiritually attack. He uses our pride to convince us, our church is the best, and our beliefs are more in line with God than the others. This divides and weakens the church. All churches should be united, teaching the Truth, and never contradicting the Bible. If you find yourself involved with a church, or religion, and the teaching contradicts the Bible, Satan will seize the opportunity to take you as deep and as dark as you will allow. Before you realize what happened, the years go by. You find you're committed to something you believe with your mind, but it has nothing to do with your heart. Once you go too deep, it can be extremely difficult to navigate your way out of this mind-set.

In spiritual warfare, Satan will use the influence of alcohol or drugs to spiritually attack. He'll take you as deep and as dark as you will allow. Before you realize what happened, you transition from alcohol or drug use, to alcohol or drug abuse. You can find yourself fighting an addiction. It can result in poor health. It can cause you to lose your job. It can destroy the closest and most loving relationships. You begin to wonder how in the world you ever allowed yourself to get into this condition. Many substance abusers and addicts will wholeheartedly declare their love for God, and have a sincere desire to make better choices. Then, soon after this life-changing declaration, they go right back to making the same bad choices. This happens because they are weak in Spirit and remain vulnerable to Satan's attacks. This is what Satan does. He looks for the opportunity to take advantage of those who are weak in Spirit. This is why, even though the bad choices you make directly conflict with what you truly desire, you are likely to give in.

Why does alcohol and drug use make us such an easy target for Satan? When under the influence, we have a tendency to respond and act differently than we would if not under the influence. We let our guard down and poor decisions are made. We get in trouble. We get mean. We get sexually promiscuous. Take a moment to look back on your life. When under the influence, do you think Satan was influencing the decisions you made, the things you said, and the things you did? Without the unrelenting spiritual attacks of Satan, would you continue to make choices that negatively affect your life and relationships? Would you keep doing the same thing over and over again? No one likes living with the memory of all the poor decisions made while under the influence. No one enjoys getting in trouble. No one enjoys performing poorly on the job. No one enjoys losing their job. If you're struggling with alcohol or drug use, it's time to face the Truth. There are spiritual forces that don't want you to make good and healthy choices. If successful, you will be distracted from a loving relationship with Christ. You will find no peace. If you need help, find help. There are people and resources available to help you. Stop allowing Satan to have the upper hand. Give the control to God. He will show you the Way.

In spiritual warfare, Satan uses our sinful nature against us. He uses our sexual desire to attack. It can lead to infidelity, sadomasochism, or homosexuality. Once you embrace this behavior, Satan will take you as deep and as dark as you will allow. Before you can realize what happened, you have years of sexual behavior that affects your mind, heart, and Spirit. You can go so deep, not only do you embrace it, but you find ways to justify it. Your sexuality becomes a way of life, a lifestyle. You begin to believe the choices you make are your right to make them. But if the choices you make conflict with what the Bible says, then you believe the lies of Satan. When you find yourself feeling guilty deep down inside, because of the decisions you've made, and the relationships destroyed, these feelings are tied to the Spirit. The Spirit is telling you one thing, while Satan is telling you another. Who are you listening to? Every decision you make has a profound influence on determining the person you become. It's not what you think and say, it's your actions that define you. The action you take becomes your reality. Are you happy with your reality?

As we examine the evil actions of individuals all around the world, can we continue to deny the existence of spiritual warfare? We've all heard the horrific stories of pedophilia within the priesthood. How many prominent members of the clergy have given in to infidelity and sexual promiscuity? If those who profess to be devout followers of Christ can be influenced and destroyed by Satan, how vulnerable are the rest of us? From mass shootings, to vehicles being used to run people over, to suicide bombings, how can the evidence of spiritual warfare be so obvious, yet we still refuse to acknowledge it? How often do we hear the term "act of pure evil" being used when the authorities can't find an apparent motive for a horrific act? Can we label something *evil* yet not admit the d*evil* is involved? We need to start doing a better job of evaluating how spiritual warfare is playing a part in these horrific acts. Some, who commit such acts, say they heard voices. Some say it was a religious cause. Some say they were mistreated, bullied, or abused as children. Some have no explanation at all for their behavior. Often, family members are shocked and claim they saw no signs of it coming.

It's time we start doing a better job of providing spiritual guidance for people who are having thoughts they don't understand, or can't control. It's time to establish an outreach, a place of compassion and understanding, where judgment is absent, and those feeling hopeless can find hope. Most everyone would immediately think the church would be a great place to find this kind of outreach. Unfortunately, not all churches are able to provide this kind of counsel. In the fallen world in which we live, the church has enough of a challenge providing guidance to those facing difficulties in marriage, finances, and raising children, because the family itself is under spiritual attack. So when it comes to spiritual warfare that is life threatening, churches are ill equipped, law enforcement can do little to prevent it, and medical facilities can only attempt to treat a diagnosed illness.

So how do we do a better job of identifying those who are spiritually struggling? How do we offer those consistently losing spiritual battles the chance to get help? How do we stop an action that someone feels compelled to act out, before it happens? We must start by acknowledging the existence of spiritual warfare and its effect on us. We must start admitting Satan can have an influence on our thoughts in a way that affects our actions. Can you believe that God the Father created us? Can you believe that Jesus lived and then died on the cross to save us? Can you believe He rose from the grave to conquer death? Then you must believe the biblical Truth that Satan exists and so does spiritual warfare. You can't believe in the Light and not in the dark. Satan is real and he is the enemy.

3

Satan, the Enemy

The existence of Satan is documented throughout the Bible. Job 1:6–7 says, "One day the members of the heavenly court came to present themselves before the LORD, and the Accuser, Satan, came with them. 'Where have you come from?' the LORD asked Satan. Satan answered the LORD, 'I have been patrolling the earth, watching everything that's going on.'" Isn't it interesting, Satan would be allowed to come before the Lord with the members of the heavenly court? Then, he uses the opportunity to tell the Lord he has been patrolling the earth, watching *everything* that's going on. Please take the time to review the book of Job. You will discover, the Lord allowed Satan to test Job. Why would God allow Satan to test Job? Does the Lord allow Satan to test us?

More documentation of Satan is found in Isaiah 14:12–15 where it says, "How you are fallen from heaven, O shining star, son of the morning! You have been thrown down to the earth, you who destroyed the nations of the world. For you said to yourself, 'I will ascend to heaven and set my throne above God's stars. I will preside on the mountain of the gods far away in the north. I will climb to the highest heavens and be like the most High.' Instead, you will be brought down to the place of the dead, down to its lowest depths." It appears Lucifer's downfall was his pride and desire to be like God. Does this sound familiar? Does our prideful demeanor make us more vulnerable to the attacks of Satan? In Luke 10:18 Jesus says, "Yes," he told them, "I saw Satan fall from heaven like lightning!" Jesus is confirming His existence, and the existence of Satan, before creation as we know it.

The continued existence of Satan and evil is evident by what we experience in our personal lives, by what we observe in the lives of those closest to us, and by what we witness going on all over the world. One of our biggest mistakes is we marginalize Satan by lightheartedly visualizing this little figure with a pitch fork and a tail. This depiction is false. There's nothing at all lighthearted about Satan. He's foul, cruel, and heartless. His spiritual presence is so massive he can patrol the earth and watch *everything* that's going on. With this kind of presence, is there any wonder why he is successful at spiritually attacking and keeping us separated from God? God is love and Satan is hate. Satan's hate is revealed in his relentless campaign of evil and darkness. He hates that we have the opportunity to be in a loving relationship with God, and he wants us to miss it. He wants us to fail, and fail miserably. He wants to foster hate within each one of us. He wants us to hate ourselves and he wants us to hate one another.

The Good News is, God created everything, including Satan. This means God is greater and more powerful than Satan. Since God allows Satan to spiritually attack us, God provides the spiritual strength we need to defend ourselves. In Acts 26:18 Jesus says, "To open their eyes, so they may turn from darkness to light and from the power of Satan to God. Then they will receive forgiveness for their sins and be given a place among God's people, who are set apart by faith in me." To turn away from darkness and the power of Satan, we must rely on the power of God, through the strength of the Holy Spirit.

Other Bible verses document the existence of Satan. In John 14:30–31 Jesus says, "I don't have much more time to talk to you, because the ruler of this world approaches. He has no power over me, but I will do what the Father requires of me, so that the world will know that I love the Father. Come, let's be going." In John 17:15, while praying to the Father, Jesus says, "I'm not asking you to take them out of the world, but to keep them safe from the evil one." In John 17:20–21 Jesus says, "I am praying not only for these disciples but also for all who will ever believe in me through their message. I pray that they will all be one, just as you and I are one—as you are in me, Father, and I am in you. And may they be in us so that the world will believe you sent me." As believers, we are included in His prayer. We are among those, *who will ever believe*, through the message of the disciples. We all need to be kept safe from the evil one. Why would Jesus pray for the disciples, and *all who will ever believe*, if it wasn't necessary?

Where do you draw the line when it comes to your belief of Satan? Do you believe the biblical documentation of Satan is true? Do you believe Satan was once an angel who rebelled against God? Do you believe Satan tempted

Eve in the garden? Do you believe God allowed Satan to test Job? Do you believe Satan tempted Jesus? If you believe Satan was present in the past, then why would you not believe he is present today? What do you think happened to him? Where does the Bible tell us he no longer exists? The Truth is he still exists. So why is Satan allowed to be present? How does he keep winning spiritual battles against us? How does he continue to succeed in keeping us from a loving relationship with God?

Paul gives witness to his own spiritual battles in Romans 7:21–25, by saying, "I have discovered this principle of life—that when I want to do what is right, I inevitably do what is wrong. I love God's law with all my heart. But there is another power within me that is at war with my mind. This power makes me a slave to the sin that is still within me. Oh, what a miserable person I am! Who will free me from this life that is dominated by sin and death? Thank God! The answer is in Jesus Christ our Lord. So you see how it is: In my mind I really want to obey God's law, but because of my sinful nature I am a slave to sin." Paul, a devoted follower of Christ, is struggling with a power within him that is at war with his mind. This gives testimony that the spiritual battle doesn't end because we decide to follow Christ. To the contrary, the battle gets more intense.

The Bible is clear in helping us to understand we are all vulnerable and inclined to follow the temptations of the devil, to disobey God and sin. First John 3:8 says, "But when people keep on sinning, it shows they belong to the devil, who has been sinning since the beginning. But the

Son of God came to destroy the works of the devil." First John 5:19 says, "We know that we are children of God and that the world around us is under control of the evil one." Ephesians 2:2 says, "You used to live in sin, just like the rest of the world, obeying the devil—the commander of the powers in the unseen world. He is the spirit at work in the hearts of those who refuse to obey God." It would be very naïve of us to see how much of the written Word is about the devil, yet still deny his existence. If you believe there is a God, you must believe that there is a devil. Simply put, you can't believe in one without the other.

Thanks to the Word of God, we have everything we need to grasp the reality of Satan, and we have everything we need to successfully fight him in spiritual battle. We have the evidence we need in both the written Word, and what we see in the world around us, to confirm that Satan exists. Satan influences the mind and heart of those who refuse to obey God. But the world has hope in the Son of God who came to destroy the works of the devil. So how does the devil continue to influence our mind to affect our heart? How does he succeed in having his way with us, and at times, completely destroying us? He's successful because we are not spiritually strong on our own. We must rely on the strength of God through the Holy Spirit. If we depend on ourselves, the devil will use our weakness against us. He will easily influence us to make ungodly decisions. If we want to stop Satan, we must improve our relationship with Christ, and rely on the strength of the Holy Spirit.

Here's how the devil uses our sinful nature against us. He is a liar. He is the Father of Lies. He'll influence us to act in a way we wouldn't normally act. He'll influence us to go ahead and have another drink or ingest more drugs, even though deep down, we know better. The next thing we know, we find ourselves in an emergency room, or a jail cell. He'll influence us to respond to flirtatious gestures that lead to inappropriate sexual encounters. The next thing we know, we're either living with the guilt and shame of indiscretion, or we think we've found the new love of our life. He'll influence us to physically or emotionally hurt others. If you find yourself becoming someone you don't recognize, there's a good chance, Satan is successfully influencing you. Furthermore, when under the influence of mind altering substances, we are even more vulnerable to his attacks. How many of us have acted in a dreadful way while under the influence? How many regrets? How much guilt? How much shame?

To win spiritual battles, we must be able to recognize when we're being attacked and immediately call on the name of the Lord. There's power in the name of Jesus Christ. It lets Satan know who's ultimately in control. Don't hesitate to tell Satan exactly how you feel. Declare you are a child of God and proclaim the power of God triumphs over the power of evil. When being attacked and influenced to do things that contradicts the Spirit, make a stand. You are on the frontline in spiritual battle. The Word of God is your truth. You don't have to memorize and quote exact Bible verses. Just start proclaiming who you are in the name of Jesus Christ. By proclaiming your dependence on God, your spiritual strength will come from a source of power like no other you have ever experienced. It's a mind boggling, heart stimulating, spiritual experience, beyond human comprehension.

This chapter may seem to be a lot of gloom and doom when it comes to Satan and how he has his way with us. But don't be discouraged. Satan never has the last word because God is the Word. God's Word says, no matter what you've done, no matter how you're labeled, you are who God says you are. As a child of God, the Father is always there for you. He desperately wants to be a part of your life, every single day. Speaking of every single day, where are we in the continuum of time, as we know it? Are we in the beginning, somewhere in the middle, or closer to the end? The Bible says we are not to know when the end is near. Mark 13:32 says, "However, no one knows the day or hour when these things will happen, not even the angels in heaven or the Son himself. Only the Father knows." Where are you in your lifespan? Are you in the beginning, some-where in the middle, or closer to the end? No matter where you are, it's not the date of your birth or the date of your death that's important, it's the dash between the two. How are you living your dash? We need to live our dash with the peace of already knowing the end of the story. God is victorious.

Have you turned your back on God? Have you been walking in the darkness for a long time? It doesn't matter. It takes a slight glance back to find God waiting for you. If you've never experienced the love of God, or you're not sure what that even means, it's very important for you to seek Him. God provides support within the church family, within your own family, among friends, in a neighbor, or even in a stranger. There are true followers of Christ available to help you walk in a new direction of healing and hope. They genuinely shine the love Light of Christ, they are non-judgmental, and they are interested in helping. But you must be willing to reach out. All it takes is a desire of the heart, a little guidance, and a lot of patience. God will take it from there.

Giving up control and learning to rely on the strength of the Holy Spirit can be very difficult. It's difficult, because the mind is the spiritual battlefield and Satan has inside knowledge. He knows when you are most vulnerable. He knows when and how to precisely attack. He gets into your psyche where he attempts to influence your choices. He'll have you going down dark paths that contradict everything you've ever wanted. Before you know what happened, you lose sight of everything most important. Satan's ability to influence your mind, ultimately affects your heart. Once he affects your heart, he has penetrated the fort.

4

The Mind Is the Battlefield, the Heart Is the Fort

God created us without the knowledge of good and evil. We acquired the knowledge as a result of the original sin, and we continue to live with that knowledge today. Throughout history, because of our sinful nature, we have continually disobeyed God. Thanks to the sacrifice of Jesus Christ on the cross, we have the opportunity to be forgiven for our sin. Thanks to the Holy Spirit, we have the opportunity to be spiritually stronger, enabling us to make better choices. But we struggle, because of our inability to reconcile our existence in the flesh, with the existence of the Spirit. It causes us to question our faith, which makes us weak in Spirit, giving Satan a foothold to influence the mind and affect the heart. It causes us to make decisions that are contrary to what God wants for us, and what we want for ourselves. If Satan is successful in his spiritual attacks, we will care less about God and the experience of the Spirit. We will care more about ourselves and the experience of the flesh.

The Good News is the power of God is greater than the power of Satan. But make no mistake about it, Satan is a spiritual power to be reckoned with, and because of our spiritual weakness, we will struggle to resist. But if we rely on the strength of the Spirit, the devil can't hold our thoughts captive. First Peter 5:8 says, "Stay alert! Watch out for your great enemy, the devil. He prowls around like a roaring lion, looking for someone to devour." This warning to stay alert is directly associated with our need to be constantly aware of a spiritually powerful attacking enemy. Our lack of awareness makes us more vulnerable to Satan's attacks and easier for him to devour. The word *devour* is specifically used to help us get a mental picture of a ruthless and brutal enemy. Take a moment to envision a ferocious lion attacking his prey with precision, to overwhelm, conquer, and devour. Now envision Satan attacking us with such precision. Not a pretty sight.

During discussions about spiritual warfare, of those who do believe in it, many say they don't believe it's a daily battle. What, Satan has an off day? Does he need a day of rest? Does he know we need a day of rest? Maybe he gives us every Sunday off to go to church and spiritually recharge. Now that sounds just like a roaring lion looking for someone to devour. Just because we're not aware of being spiritually attacked, it doesn't mean it's not happening. We're a part of a much bigger spiritual picture, and we're not aware of everything that's going on in the spiritual realm. Ephesians 6:12 says, "For we are not fighting against flesh-and-blood enemies, but against evil rulers and authorities of the unseen world, against mighty powers in this dark world, and against evil spirits in the heavenly places." A little scary when you add an enemy who devours like a lion, right? But don't be afraid, the power of God is greater than the power of Satan.

Have you ever wondered why you wake up in the worst mood, and there's no apparent reason? You go all day and you just can't shake it. You feel depressed, somber, unmotivated, and lethargic. Then, on other days you wake up in the best mood, feeling great. You go all day feeling uplifted, motivated, inspired, and enthused. These mood swings can be influenced by illness, medication, diet, or stress. But when there seems to be no obvious reason, it could be spiritual. Do you ever think strange or random thoughts and have no clue where they came from? Do you get distracted when trying to focus on important things like school, work, or reading the Bible? When contemplating important decisions, do you ever lose focus, and wonder where that came from? It's obviously not your desire to lose focus, so where do you think these distractions come from? It could be Satan distracting you. So, as soon as you become aware of the distraction, immediately take the control back in the name of the Lord. Taking the control back in the name of Christ is a spiritual power play. It shows the devil that you're aware of your need to depend on God for spiritual strength. It lets him know you're ready, willing, and able to fight.

Do you find yourself making choices, even though in your mind and heart, you know they're wrong? Despite the fact you acknowledge that gut feeling deep inside, you do it anyway. Then, after the results of your decisions unfold, you know the choices you made were in conflict with what you preferred. This inner feeling, usually felt deep down in the pit of your stomach, suggests the spiritual battle within. The spiritual battle between good and evil exists between a thought and an action. Our response to the spiritual attacks, and our willingness to engage, ultimately influences our decisions. After a decision is made, a direction in life is taken, and it becomes our reality. Our reality is a culmination of every spiritual battle we encounter and every decision we make.

Why do we feel guilty? Why can't we just make a choice and live with it? Guilt is the emotional response to making ungodly decisions, knowing we had the opportunity to choose differently. Just think if we didn't have the feeling of guilt? Would we do whatever we want? Would everyone just take from one another? Would we hurt or kill people without a second thought? This guiltless scenario is a lesson from the past. Our history reminds us of the days when it was conquer or be conquered, and only the strong survived. But thanks to God's love, grace, mercy, and forgiveness, we evolved into God-fearing people. But even as God-fearing people, Satan still successfully influences many of us to act on our desires to conquer. We take things that don't belong to us. We harm others.

The evidence of Satan's influence is witnessed by all the hate and evil in the world. To combat this, we must rely on the strength of the Holy Spirit, sent to help us make better choices, to serve, love, and care for one another, and to love and serve God. We also have the freedom to make choices despite how the Spirit moves in us. Even though we know deep down that something doesn't feel right, we can ignore the feeling, do what we want anyway, and suffer the consequences. The consequences of ignoring the Spirit is witnessed in what we see going on all over the world.

Every day we are challenged by a multitude of spiritually influenced choices that profoundly affect our lives. Good and evil, positive and negative, any way you want to frame it, there are unseen spiritual forces vying for our attention. The spiritual conflict that takes place in the brain during the decision-making process is what makes the mind the battlefield. If our focus becomes about immediate gratification, usually tied to earthly pleasures, Satan will win that battle. If our focus becomes about the Spirit and what God wants for our lives, we will win that battle. The decisions we make and the action we take ultimately affect the heart.

Paul says in Ephesians 2:1–2, "Once you were dead because of your disobedience and your many sins. You used to live in sin, just like the rest of the world, obeying the devil—the commander of the powers of the unseen world. He is the spirit at work in the hearts of those who refuse to obey God." Paul is teaching us that if we are not obeying God, we are obeying the devil. Our disobedience gives the devil the opportunity to affect the heart, which means he's penetrating the fort. Once he penetrates the fort and gets a foothold, he'll successfully influence you for as long as you allow.

As we examine the condition of the world and what we continue to witness, can we deny the devil has a foothold on the hearts of many? Can we deny the evil associated with the amount of alcohol, drug, spousal, child, and elderly abuse? Can we deny the evil associated with the hatred and rage in response to religion, skin color, sexual preference, and politics? Watch the news, surf the internet, or simply observe other people and the choices being made. Do we see the love of God, or the hate of Satan? God is love, the devil is hate. So when an individual embraces evil, and their actions affect innocent bystanders, it exposes the devil. Evil creates consequences for others who had no idea that something was about to happen. In an instant, innocent lives can be changed forever. It may be as random as an enraged driver encountered on the road. Or it can be as elaborate as a planned terrorist attack.

As we examine the condition of the family, our inner circle of friends, neighbors, acquaintances, our towns and cities, we can see the devil has a foothold. We can see how Satan is influencing the decisions of individuals within those factions. Although we are personally responsible for every decision we make in our lives, how quick we are to blame everyone else. It wasn't my fault. Another person influenced me. I was in the wrong place at the wrong time. I'm a product of my upbringing. The drugs made me do it. The alcohol made me do it. The devil made me do it. The devil can't make you do anything. He can only attempt to influence behavior. How about friends who lead others astray by influencing them to make a bad decision? There are so many life-changing decisions, made in a split-second, resulting in horrific life-changing consequences.

Are we naturally predisposed to sin? You bet we are. In the beginning, Adam and Eve were created in the image of

God to live forever in a close and personal relationship with Him. But for some reason, and God only knows, Satan was allowed to be present in the garden. He had one purpose for being there, to wedge himself between us and God. The rest, as they say, is history. Because of Satan and his evil schemes, and our failure to obey God, we were destined to live in a fallen world, a world of suffering and decay. We continue to live in this fallen world, but there's a major difference between then and now. Now, we have a Savior named Jesus Christ. Because God knew we could not save ourselves, He sent His Son to save us. Jesus lived a sinless life in the flesh, to become the perfect and final sacrifice for our sins. Thanks to His sacrifice, we once again have the opportunity to be in a close and personal relationship with God. After His death, Christ ascended back to heaven, and the Father sent the Holy Spirit to live in all who believe.

This sets the scene for our current existence in this fallen world. Today, we spend an enormous amount of time being distracted by technology. We spend most of our time watching television, surfing the internet, texting and talking on the phone. Because we focus more on the things of this world, and less on the things of the Spirit, Satan uses this opportunity to spiritually attack. The distractions of this world allow Satan to influence our behavior, because we don't give much thought to the spiritual realm, and we are easily defeated in spiritual battle. The devil will use every means available to spiritually attack us. He'll do anything and everything within his power to influence us to disobey God. He'll use alcohol, drugs, lust, desire, lies, worry, depression, and pride, to get at us. He'll use absolutely anything to distract us from a personal relationship with God. If he can separate us from God, he can have his way with us. So he attacks with precision, specific to each of us. His attacks are designed to influence the mind, at exactly the right time, when we are most vulnerable. The Bible refers to the weapons he uses as the fiery arrows.

5

The Fiery Arrows
of the Devil

The devil is spiritual, so his attacks are spiritual. But his spiritual attacks can affect both our spiritual and physical health. Therefore, our physical sickness is often a reflection of our spiritual sickness. How much physical damage has been inflicted as a result of drug, alcohol, sex, and food addiction? How much physical illness is self-inflicted as a result of the unhealthy spiritual and physical choices we make? If you wonder how true this is, look around at all the walking wounded. Our only hope of combatting the spiritual attacks of Satan is through our faith in Jesus Christ, and our dependence on the strength of the Spirit.

So how does Satan spiritually attack us? The Bible refers to the weapons the devil attacks us with, as the fiery arrows. Ephesians 6:16 says, "In addition to all of these, hold up the shield of faith to stop the fiery arrows of the devil." Since faith is our shield, in an effort to weaken us, Satan attempts to wedge himself between us and God. He targets whatever he perceives as our weakness, in an attempt to influence us to do things that will negatively affect our lives. If he successfully separates us from God, we will be weak in faith. If our faith is weak, our shield is weak, and Satan's fiery arrows will have more of an effect on us. When we combine our sinful nature with the influence of Satan, we can find ourselves doing more of what Satan wants, and less of what the Spirit wants.

Because the devil has insight into our weakness and his attacks are personal and strategic, it would be impossible for the Bible to list all the fiery arrows available. He attacks at just the right time, with just the right arrow, when we are most vulnerable. Satan uses our emotional condition and our spiritual sickness to influence us to make decisions we would prefer not to make.

What are some of the more obvious fiery arrows the devil uses to attack? There's the fiery arrow of doubt. Satan shoots the fiery arrows of doubt when we, or someone we know, gets gravely ill. Doubt causes us to question God's purpose or intention. We begin to question our faith, and at times, whether there is even a God at all. If the sickness involves an innocent child, we can easily find ourselves going deep with Satan. After all, why in the world would God allow an innocent child to get sick? Why would God allow anyone to suffer?

If we lose our job, Satan will shoot the fiery arrows of doubt, influencing us to question why God would allow this to happen. Satan will use doubt to influence us to question our worthiness. We can find ourselves losing hope of ever finding another job. As our doubt becomes stronger, our faith becomes weaker. We become even more vulnerable to Satan's attacks. We can find ourselves turning to earthly fixes like drugs and alcohol. Not only do we have the things we're already having trouble dealing with, but now we've added self-medication to the problem. Because Satan is ruthless and relentless, he keeps the fiery arrows coming.

The lack of self-confidence is a common reaction to the fiery arrows of doubt. Satan will influence you to think, who do you think you are? You'll never amount to anything. If you failed once, you'll surely fail again. You'll never achieve your goals and dreams. He'll influence you to settle for less, and completely stop trying. He'll influence you to believe the other person got the job because you're not worthy. In reality, the other person got the job because God was blessing them at the time. He'll remind you of all your past relationships that didn't work out. Even if you didn't act right and share the blame, he'll have you believing it was entirely your fault.

He'll use pride to mask your lack of confidence. He'll influence you to think, the hell with the world if it doesn't accept you. He'll tell you to just keep being who you are, and don't let anyone change you. He'll have you convinced, you couldn't change if you wanted to. Here's the Truth. Everyone needs to change and everyone can change. If we're not changing, we're not developing, and we're not spiritually transforming into the person God wants us to be. We need to transform from less of an existence of the flesh, to more of an existence of the Spirit. This spiritual transformation continues our entire life.

There are the fiery arrows of guilt. Guilt is an emotional response associated with the thoughts and feelings resulting from choices we're ashamed of. It can come from something we do and instantly regret or it can come from something we did in our past. Either way, Satan will fire an onslaught of the fiery arrows of guilt because he wants us to keep thinking about and reliving the sins of our past. He wants to use our guilt to make us feel unworthy of God's forgiveness.

Watch out, Satan is the master manipulator. He'll convert your feelings of guilt into feelings of pride. He'll have you thinking and acting like you don't care and it doesn't matter. He'll use your guilt to keep you distant from God. He'll influence you to turn away from the Light and walk toward the darkness. He'll convince you, that you're not worthy of God's love. He'll have you questioning the love of those closest to you. He'll have you pulling away from those who love you most. He wants to isolate you, and shoot you with so many fiery arrows of guilt, that you'll be overwhelmed with the darkness of depression.

Our feelings of guilt come from the Spirit when we disobey God. When we have inappropriate thoughts, we feel guilty. When we are unkind, or turn our back on someone in need, we feel guilty. We feel guilty when we are rude, lose our temper, or patience. The devil will use our feelings of guilt to condemn us. He'll tell us we're losers and unworthy. He'll have us convinced, it's not our fault, and we can't help ourselves. To some degree, he's right; we can't help ourselves. To protect ourselves from the fiery arrows of guilt, we must rely on the strength of the Spirit to faithfully believe in the grace and forgiveness of Jesus Christ.

Satan knows if we continue to feel guilty, we really haven't accepted the forgiveness of God, and we will remain weak in Spirit. He'll keep stirring up thoughts and feelings associated with the sins of our past. He wants us to emotionally relive the same sin over and over again. Have you noticed when you're continuing to own the guilt from your past sin, it feels similar to how it emotionally felt when the sin first took place? It doesn't matter whether it was last year or twenty years ago. The guilt from your past will negatively affect your mind, heart, and Spirit, in the present.

If you're currently walking in the Light and making good decisions, the devil will bring up the darkness from your past, because the past is all he has to work with. Out of nowhere, you'll randomly recall the things you've done you're not proud of. Some you completely forgot about. Don't let Satan use your past against you. The Bible tells you God is faithful to forgive you. Don't let the devil get away with influencing your present with your past sin. First John 1:9 says, "But if we confess our sins to him, he is faithful and just to forgive us our sins and cleanse us from all wickedness." God washes away our sin with the shed blood of Jesus. He provides the opportunity for a new beginning.

When sinful behavior knocks us down, God's forgiveness picks us up. When sinful behavior results in setbacks that seem hopeless, God moves us forward, with the hope of Jesus Christ. God wants us to learn from our past and become stronger for it. He wants to use our past struggle to help us grow stronger in Spirit. Satan doesn't want us to accept God's forgiveness and find hope in Jesus Christ. He doesn't want us to experience the love of God, or enjoy His peace. He wants us to live with the compounded guilt of every single sin. He'll use our guilt to overwhelm us and negatively affect our spiritual and physical well-being. He'll use it to sever our personal relationship with Christ and destroy our earthly relationships. Satan knows if we feel guilty, unworthy, and defeated, he'll have us right where he wants us.

Along with the fiery arrows of guilt, Satan shoots the fiery arrows of shame. Shame comes when we make a decision to do something that results in embarrassment, dishonor, or disgrace, to ourselves, or those we care about. Satan will influence us to think we'll never get through this, or get over that. He'll keep shooting those fiery arrows of shame to keep reminding us of what we did. He wants us to keep living the same shame, and the emotional pain, over and over again. Because of what we've done, he wants us to believe, we're not worthy of God's love.

Are you living today with the emotional pain of past shame? Are you living with the shame of something that wasn't even your fault, something not within your control? Do you want to turn the tables on Satan? Every time he brings up your past to make you feel shame, take that opportunity while it's fresh in your mind, to once and for all, give it to God. You can even go a step further. Ask God to help you recall all your past sin you may not remember. You'll be surprised at what comes to mind. As you recall the sin of your past, lean on the strength of the Spirit to know you are forgiven. Stop reading and do this right now. Ask the Holy Spirit for help. Sit and be quiet. Listen.

Now, when the devil brings up the sins from your past, chances are, you've already dealt with them. He can no longer catch you off guard. Acts 3:19 says, "Now repent of your sins and turn to God, so that your sins may be wiped away." Colossians 1:13–14 says, "For he has rescued us from the kingdom of darkness and transferred us into the Kingdom of his dear Son, who purchased our freedom and forgave our sins." Psalm 103:12 says, "He has removed our sins as far from us as the east is from the west." Don't let the lies of Satan keep you from the forgiveness the Savior paid so dearly for.

There are the fiery arrows of anger. Are you mad at yourself? Are you mad at the world? Do you blame the world for all your troubles? Do you blame everyone else for your troubles? Anger causes us to hold grudges that damage and sever loving relationships. How many of us get upset and justify reasons to continue to hold a grudge against someone? Some grudges last a lifetime. Who hurts most when we hold a grudge? Some people we hold grudges against, aren't even aware we're still holding them. To compound anger, Satan shoots an onslaught of the fiery arrows of rage. Rage is uncontrolled anger. It's unhealthy, and at times dangerous. It's the face of evil. The next time you get really angry, put your face close to a mirror. It's a very revealing reflection of evil.

There are the fiery arrows of hate. God is love, and Satan opposes God's love with hate. Because of our sinful nature, we are easily influenced to hate. Love is difficult, because it requires more effort. Relationships fail because it's easier to walk away from them than it is to work on them. The reality of this can be found in how many severed relationships there are within the family, and how many failed marriages. Do you blame yourself for your failed relationships, or do you blame everyone else? Should it really matter who's to blame?

How about your relationship with Christ? Do you blame God for your failed relationship with Him? Do you blame Him for everything that goes wrong in your life? Do you find reasons to hate God? Do you find it easy to cuss God, and use His name in vain? Do you hate the fact everything doesn't always go the way you think it should, and you don't have all the answers? How many times a day do you use the word hate? I hate him. I hate her. I hate them. I hate this. I hate that. I hate what they said. I hate what they did. How many fiery arrows of hate is the devil shooting at you? How many are successfully landing?

There are the fiery arrows of jealousy or envy. Jealousy is an emotional response that causes us to act in an unflattering, and ungodly way. It's often unfounded and results in false accusations. It questions motives. It causes relationships to suffer and fail. How many relationships and marriages have failed because of jealousy? Walking hand in hand with jealousy is envy. We can be envious of what someone else has. We can envy their house or car. We can envy their job. We can envy someone's relationship with their spouse, siblings, or kids. From the outside looking in, the grass always seems greener on the other side. It can appear like someone is as happy as can be, but in reality, they are struggling with the same things we're struggling with. Everyone is fighting their own onslaught of the fiery arrows of envy. Satan is fully aware, no matter what we have, or what we achieve, most are never satisfied. We want more, something bigger, and something better. We need to stop envying what we don't have, and find satisfaction in what we do have. Until we are able to thank God for the many blessings, Satan will keep shooting the fiery arrows of jealousy and envy. We will never be happy, we will never find peace.

There are the fiery arrows of bitterness and resentment. There's the thought of, why me? Why am I sick? Why is my father or mother sick? Why does my brother or sister struggle so much? Why does my kid continue to get in trouble? Why didn't I get the job? Why did I lose my job? Why am I always living paycheck to paycheck? Satan wants us to think we always get the short end of the stick. He wants us to focus on what we don't have, rather than what we do have. He never wants us to be satisfied or content. He wants us to be bitter and resentful. He wants us to see our glass half empty, instead of half full. When we focus on what we don't have, we develop a spirit of bitterness and resentment. When we focus on what we do have, we develop a Spirit of thankfulness.

There are the fiery arrows of idolatry. First John 5:19–21 says, "We know that we are children of God and that the world around us is under the control of the evil one. And we know that the Son of God has come, and he has given us understanding so that we can know the true God. And now we live in fellowship with the true God because we live in fellowship with his Son, Jesus Christ. He is the only true God, and he is eternal life. Dear children, keep away from anything that might take God's place in your hearts." When anything of this world becomes more important to us than God, we are engaging in idolatry. It distracts us from developing a personal relationship with Christ, and it reveals our true heart.

Now let's get real. There's nothing wrong with enjoying the things of this world. Matter of fact, God blesses us with the things of this world to enjoy. We can enjoy having money, nice clothes, transportation, a place to call home, or a well-deserved vacation. We can enjoy the sports and the athletes, the music and the artists, the movies and the actors. There's nothing wrong with enjoying all that life has to offer. The problem comes when we allow the things of this world to become more important to us than God. When it's easier to say we love the things of this world, than it is to say we love God, we have a spiritual problem.

When we lift up celebrities and place them on a pedestal, we are in essence giving them permission to act as though they are godlike, idols in fact. Our reaction to celebrities encourages them to think they are more important than they really are. It produces arrogant and prideful behavior. We encourage their behavior by spending our hard-earned money on the products they produce. How many actually deserve our continued support? Our support encourages more of the same behavior. We empower them. Once we empower them, Satan uses the fiery arrows to attack them. They begin to believe they have all the answers. They can't wait to share their personal opinion on anything and everything, and quite frankly, we can't wait to hear it. They think they know everything from how to run the country to what religious belief we should all embrace.

When celebrities use their popularity to influence how we think, we should be especially cautious.

Here's the reality. Celebrities struggle with the same things we struggle with. Their lives and relationships are just as challenging. Look at all the failed marriages and relationships involving celebrities. How many experience difficulties as a result of drugs and alcohol? Having money and success can seemingly be quite euphoric in its affects, but in reality, it can negatively impact one's life. Money and success don't make you wise, respecting and working the process is what makes you wise. When a person's celebrity status defines who they are, they become more about the hype, and less about the person God intended them to be.

We are all passing through this life, and we all make choices. When someone becomes successful, he or she should not be catapulted into a godlike status. This god-like status often translates into unacceptable behavior and the offering of opinions not within their level of expertise. Watch out for these people, for they are beacons of false hope. There are some celebrities who never hesitate to give all the glory to God. Hopefully these celebrities will continue to be blessed and become beacons of hope for others pursuing similar dreams.

If you want insight into whether you've allowed Satan and the things of this world to take God's place in your heart, answer these questions. How much time a day, a week, or a month do you spend on the computer, phone, or watching TV? In comparison, how much time a day, a week, or a month do you spend with God? How much time do you dedicate to spiritual development, reading and studying the Bible? How much time do you spend praying or just talking with God? How much time do you spend just being quiet with God? How involved are you with the church? Do you attend Sunday service out of guilt, or do you look forward to the experience? What do you conclude from your answers? Most would conclude they need to do better. The Good News is it's never too late. Start making better use of your time. Start spending more time with God.

Satan uses the fiery arrows of fear to spiritually attack. Fear can paralyze, causing us to fall short of attaining our goals and dreams, or to ignore God's calling and God's purpose for our life. Fear can cause us to stop trying and to give up. Sometimes we can find ourselves so deep in the pit of despair that we have difficulty just crawling out. We can become so accustomed to how we feel; we accept our reality as our fate, our destiny.

Satan uses fear to keep us within our self-perceived, self-imposed comfort zone. Instead, we should be using the power of the Holy Spirit to set ourselves free from fear, to step out of our comfort zone. We need to combat fear to fulfill the plans God has for our lives. We need to spend more time being thankful and less time complaining. We should be professing our love for God and our dependence on Him. When we are fearless in the way we show our love for God, it gives other people an opportunity to see our Light. We should not allow fear to keep us from shining our Light. We are all responsible to further the Kingdom of God.

Our fear of failure is one of the most prominent reasons why we don't try. When we make the effort to do something and it doesn't work out, we often respond by quitting. This is exactly what Satan wants. He doesn't want us to succeed, he wants us to fail. When we are defeated and down, he keeps shooting the fiery arrows of fear. He'll have us believing we can't do it, we're not good enough, and we're not worthy. To combat fear, we must rely on the strength of the Spirit for courage. Philippians 4:13 says, "For I can do everything through Christ, who gives me strength." If it's God's will we succeed down the path of our choosing, He'll provide the way, at the right time. We will find strength and assurance through the Holy Spirit to help us recognize with increased confidence, we can accomplish the things God wants us to accomplish. Here's the key. His will, His timing, His way. Proverbs 16:9 says, "We can make our plans, but the Lord determines our steps."

The fiery arrow of worry is the ultimate mind game the devil uses against us. Worry is the byproduct of our attempt to control the things in our life we don't have control over. We not only worry about our own life, we worry about the lives of those around us. We have well intended motives, and truly want what's best for everyone, but worry doesn't help anyone. Worry creates mental anxiety that can make us physically sick. Because of the mental and physical effects, worry is one of the most effective ways for the devil to keep us down. He'll ultimately defeat us in mind, body, and Spirit. No matter the circumstances, the devil will use worry to keep us from finding joy in our life. Even when everything seems to be going well, the devil will help us find something to worry about. It becomes habitual. It becomes a way of life. Worry can cause us to overstep boundaries in an attempt to fix the problems of other people. It can alienate us from the people we care most about. It can ruin relationships.

Worry affects other parts of our life that's not even related to what we were worrying about in the first place. When we are down, upset, or concerned about one aspect of our life, we allow worry to spill over into other parts of our life. We quit having fun, we stop getting together with friends and family. We start alienating ourselves and allow worry to negatively impact our Spirit. Before we know it, worry becomes more of who we are, than what we do. Satan wants us to be a worrier; God wants us to be a warrior. We must become a warrior in spiritual battle. We need to take up the fight and battle Satan in his attempts to use the fiery arrows of worry against us. We do this by giving the worry and the control to God. Jesus says in Matthew 6:25, "That is why I tell you not to worry about everyday life—whether you have enough food and drink, or enough clothes to wear. Isn't life more than food, and your body more than clothing?" Philippians 4:6–7 says, "Don't worry about anything; instead, pray about everything. Tell God what you need, and thank him for all he has done. Then you will experience God's peace, which exceeds anything we can understand. His peace will guard your hearts and minds as you live in Christ Jesus." Which do you prefer? Do you want to worry, or do you want peace?

When you find yourself worrying, replace your thoughts of worry with thoughts of thankfulness. A thankful Spirit finds God's peace. Although the Bible is very adamant about us not worrying, we still do it. If we continue to worry, instead of giving the control to God, we are failing to obey God. First Peter 5:6–7 says, "So humble yourselves under the mighty power of God, and at the right time he will lift you up in honor. Give all your worries and cares to God, for he cares about you." When we don't humble ourselves, and give the control to God, we are being prideful. Humility is the opposite of pride. We can know God's power, and experience His peace, by humbly giving the control to Him.

Looking back on your life, what problems has worry actually solved? Has worry ever accomplished anything at all? What positive effect has worry had on your problems, or the problems of the people you worried about? Has your worry ever fixed anything? Worry is all emotion and no action. We are created to exist in a world dependent upon God, so why do we insist on depending on ourselves? We can be free from anxiety and worry, so why do we insist on taking on all this worry that causes undue stress? Aren't we overwhelmed enough with the things we actually do control? Identify the things you try to control, but shouldn't. Give that control to God and let Him take some of the stress away. Just give it away. Satan knows that if we stop worrying and start putting our trust in God, we will learn to rely more on Him. He knows if we rely more on God, our relationship with God will strengthen and become a barrier to his attacks. So he keeps launching the fiery arrows of worry.

If we look at the world around us, it's no wonder we struggle with worry. We worry about our health, our job, our family, our children, our schools, our government, and our country. We worry about the uprising of hate all around the world. We worry about so many things we absolutely have no control over. Jesus says in Luke 12:25–26, "Can all your worries add a single moment to your life? And if worry can't accomplish a little thing like that, what's the use of worrying over bigger things?" In Luke 12:31 Jesus says, "Seek the Kingdom of God above all else, and he will give you everything you need."

Satan relentlessly shoots the fiery arrows of worry to keep us from finding peace with God. He wants to make us sick. He wants to depress us by making us continuously think about the things we can't control. He influences us to feel responsible for fixing the problems of those we care about. In an attempt to combat the feeling of despair that accompanies worry, we find ourselves turning to alcohol, medication, or illegal drugs to find peace. Even as we attempt to help ourselves with earthly fixes, we continue to worry, because the devil doesn't stop firing his arrows. The devil now has us worrying about everything we worried about before, but he's added the despair that self-medication brings. Nothing gets fixed, and we're even further away from God than before.

Hopefully you have gained insight and understanding as to why it would be impossible to list every fiery arrow Satan will use to attack. His attacks are personal and he attacks with precision. His fiery arrows are specifically designed to target where and when we are most vulnerable.

Because spiritual warfare is too complex and abstract for us to fully understand, God has provided the battle plan we need to fight in spiritual battle.

6

The Battle Plan

In physical warfare, the most brilliant military minds provide the battle plans needed to successfully fight and win battles. The success of these plans depends on how well they are carried out. In spiritual warfare, God provides the battle plan needed to successfully fight and win battles. The success of His plan also depends on how well the plans are carried out. Everything we need to know has been provided in God's Word.

Before we get into the plan itself, we must first understand the need for the plan today. The spiritual sickness of the world today is no different now, than it was when Paul first revealed the plan. Paul says in Ephesians 2:1–2, "Once you were dead because of your disobedience and your many sins. You used to live in sin, just like the rest of the world, obeying the devil—the commander of the powers in the unseen world. He is the spirit at work in the hearts of those who refuse to obey God." Although Paul was writing in the present, God was also using Paul to write to us, in the future.

Are we any different today? Isn't the commander of the powers in the unseen world still at work in the hearts of those who refuse to obey God? In Ephesians 2:3, Paul continues by saying, "All of us used to live that way, following the passionate desires and inclinations of our sinful nature. By our very nature we were subject to God's anger, just like everyone else." Isn't this true? Didn't we all used to live that way? Then in Ephesians 2:4–5, Paul reveals some Good News by saying, "But God is so rich in mercy, and he loved us so much, that even though we were dead because of our sins, he gave us life when he raised Christ from the dead. (It is only by God's grace that you have been saved!)" This same Good News applies to us today, as it did when originally written.

God provides the spiritual battle plan because Satan's attacks are spiritual, and we don't have the knowledge, or the spiritual strength, to fight on our own. Satan wants to influence us to turn away from the Light and stay in the darkness, where we will follow the passionate desires, and the inclinations of our sinful nature. As followers of Christ, Satan knows we've been there, done that, and he wants us back. As potential followers of Christ, Satan wants to keep us right where he has us.

Without the spiritual battle plan from God, we are not capable of defending ourselves from an attacking spiritual enemy. The battle plan provides the knowledge we need to be prepared. Ephesians 6:10 says, "A final word: Be strong in the Lord and in his mighty power." Paul is emphasizing the need to rely on God's strength and power. Ephesians 6:11 says, "Put on all God's armor so that you will be able to stand firm against all strategies of the devil." To stand firm against all the strategies of the devil, Paul is stressing the importance of putting on every single piece of God's armor. Absolutely nothing can be left off.

Ephesians 6:12 says, "For we are not fighting against flesh-and-blood enemies, but against evil rulers and authorities of the unseen world, against mighty powers in this dark world, and against evil spirits in the heavenly places." That sounds unreal, not of this world, right? Wrong. It's real, and the devil has the ability to influence this world. He has one mission, and that is to get between us and God. He's ruthless, cruel, nasty, and foul. He's relentless and unyielding. Ephesians 6:13 says, "Therefore, put on every piece of God's armor so you will be able to resist the enemy in the time of evil. Then after the battle you will still be standing firm."

Imagine a soldier preparing for physical battle, who fails to put on every single piece of armor available. That would be a major mistake. It would also be a major mistake for us to fail to put on every piece of God's armor. Ephesians 6:14 says, "Stand your ground, putting on the belt of truth and the body armor of God's righteousness." The belt of Truth enables us to stand our ground, knowing the Word of God is true. The body armor of God's righteousness refers to being made right through our faith in Jesus Christ. Ephesians 6:15 says, "For shoes, put on the peace that comes from the Good News so that you will be fully prepared." When was the last time you were at peace? Are you fully prepared?

Ephesians 6:16 says, "In addition to all of these, hold up the shield of faith to stop the fiery arrows of the devil." If faith is our shield, how many people in the world today are more vulnerable to the attacks of Satan because they lack faith? Ephesians 6:17 says, "Put on salvation as your helmet, and take the sword of the Spirit, which is the word of God." Salvation listed as the helmet is an important point. The mind is the battlefield, so it's just as important to protect the head in spiritual battle as it is in physical battle. So what's the significance of the helmet associated with salvation? It's because salvation, knowing we are saved and have spiritual life eternal with God, eliminates the fear of death in this life.

The final piece of God's armor is the only offensive weapon listed. It's the sword of the Spirit, the Word of God. Christ used the Word of God when He was tempted by the devil in the wilderness. Although He is God, and had so many resources available to use against Satan, He used the Word of God. He did this to show us that we too need to use the Word of God as a weapon when we are tempted by the devil. That's why Paul called it the sword of the Spirit.

During the time the Bible was written, physical warfare was common, so Paul used descriptive war terms to help us understand spiritual warfare. Although physical warfare is not as common today, we can still understand everything Paul is saying. He is saying that spiritual warfare is as real as physical warfare, and we must take an active role in defending ourselves. Just as in physical warfare, in spiritual warfare there is intelligence and counterintelligence. As we study the Bible we gain intelligence. At the same time, Satan is gaining counterintelligence on us. He knows our weakness and vulnerabilities. He strategically attacks when we are weak in Spirit and more susceptible to embrace the sin in our lives.

The sin in our lives directly impacts our spiritual and physical condition, and Satan uses both against us. He will use our brokenness to squelch the Light within us. He keeps attacking in an attempt to cause us to spiral out of control, into the darkness. Once in the darkness, Satan wants to keep us there and continue to have his way with us. We need to study the Bible to become more knowledgeable, but more important, we must believe the knowledge. The Truth leads to faith, and faith is our shield. No matter what Satan throws at us, we always have the Good News, God loves us and He is always with us. Romans 8:38–39 says, "And I am convinced that nothing can ever separate us from God's love. Neither death nor life, neither angels nor demons, neither our fears for today nor our worries about tomorrow—not even the powers of hell can separate us from God's love. No power in the sky above or in the earth below—indeed, nothing in all creation will ever be able to separate us from the love of God that is revealed in Christ Jesus our Lord." What else can be said here? Nothing can separate us from the love of God that is revealed in Christ Jesus our Lord. Now that's an amazing Truth.

The collateral damage associated with losing spiritual battles is mental and physical suffering. If we look around at the world today, we see all the wounding and suffering. To minimize the wounding and suffering, we must prepare and train for battle. We need to study the plan. We need to practice putting on all God's armor. Even with studying and practicing, we will not win every spiritual battle. But what's most important is to learn from every battle, and then apply what we learn to become spiritually stronger for it. If we get knocked down, we must rely on God's strength to get back up. Once we successfully get back up, we have even more confidence.

The importance of understanding God's Word cannot be overstated. He knows we need it, and He provides the wisdom to succeed. Without the wisdom of God, we remain weak in Spirit and vulnerable to the attacks of Satan. We will be defeated in spiritual battle, which will result in setbacks, failure, and for some, ultimate destruction. It will negatively affect our earthly relationships, but more importantly, it will affect our personal relationship with God. How well we are protected, is dependent upon our faith. The size of our faith is equal to the size of our shield. This is why we need to develop faith. We need to spend more time with God and His Word. We need to gain a better understanding of who He is. Our time devoted to studying His Word will bring about more meaning and understanding. We will experience His love, His strength, and His peace.

If you find yourself losing faith and drifting toward the darkness, don't despair. The Light shines brightest in the darkness. We must never stop believing that God knows everything and He is everywhere. He embraces us in the dark to walk us out of the darkness, and back into the Light.

You might be overwhelmed at the thought of Satan actually being able to spiritually attack. You may doubt that you have the faith and spiritual strength you need to battle such an enemy. But here's more Good News. Just as God provides the battle plan, He also provides the strength of the Holy Spirit.

7

The Holy Spirit

As we go through life and the challenges it brings, we can find ourselves becoming very frustrated and at times overwhelmed. Sometimes it can feel as if we are doing our best just to survive. We accept most of what happens as coincidence, luck, fate, or destiny. Then, when we consider God as a part of our life, we get even more frustrated, because we can't grasp or understand why certain things happen in our life. Why are there so many unanswered questions? We feel this way because we lack faith. Without faith, we fail to recognize, acknowledge, and interact with the Holy Spirit. Without tapping into the strength of the Spirit, we lack spiritual inspiration and motivation. We have difficulty knowing and feeling God's love.

Because God knew our need, the Father sent the Holy Spirit. With the strength of the Spirit, we no longer have to depend on just our own strength. In John 14:15–17, Jesus promises the Holy Spirit by saying, "If you love me, obey my commandments. And I will ask the Father, and he will give you another Advocate, who will never leave you. He is the Holy Spirit, who leads into all truth. The world cannot receive him, because it isn't looking for him and doesn't recognize him. But you know him, because he lives with you now and later will be in you." Do you love Jesus? Do you obey His commandments? Are you looking for the Holy Spirit? Do you recognize Him? Do you believe the Holy Spirit is in *you*?

God sent the Holy Spirit to guide, support, and comfort us through our entire lives. So as we struggle with the challenges and the frustrations of life, we must learn to rely on the strength of the Spirit. The Holy Spirit will not only help us to get through our challenges, He will help us to be more successful at living life to the fullest. As we learn to depend more on the Spirit, we develop more faith, trust, and peace. We will begin to gain more insight into what life's really all about.

The Word of God tells us the Holy Spirit is one of three parts of the Trinity. There's God the Father, God the Son, and God the Holy Spirit. Although there is only one God, there are three distinct parts with distinct responsibilities. God the Father, spoke everything into existence, and created man to be in a personal relationship with Him. He then created woman to be in a personal relationship with man. This gives us insight and understanding that God is a God of relationship. God the Son, descended to Earth to be born of a virgin, to walk among us in the flesh, and to become the final sacrifice for our sins. A sacrifice that only the Son of God was capable of fulfilling. Hebrews 2:14 says, "Because God's children are human beings—made of flesh and blood—the Son also became flesh and blood. For only as a human being could he die, and only by dying could he break the power of the devil, who had the power of death."

The Son of God had to die in the flesh and be resurrected from the grave, to break the power of the devil and death. After His death, Jesus purposely appeared to the apostles for forty days to confirm He was alive. Acts 1:3 says, "During the forty days after he suffered and died, he appeared to the apostles from time to time, and he proved to them in many ways that he was actually alive. And he talked to them about the Kingdom of God." In Acts 1:8–9 Jesus says, "But you will receive power when the Holy Spirit comes upon you. And you will be my witnesses, telling people about me everywhere—in Jerusalem, throughout Judea, in Samaria, and to the ends of the earth. After saying this, he was taken up into a cloud while they were watching, and they could no longer see him." In John 14:26 Jesus says, "But when the Father sends the Advocate as my representative—that is, the Holy Spirit—he will teach you everything and will remind you of everything I have told you." What a wonderful promise. He will teach us everything and He will remind us of everything Jesus told us. As part of this teaching and reminding, the writers of the Bible were inspired by the Holy Spirit. This emphasizes the importance of why we must study the Word, and adhere to its teachings.

Because of how much He loves us, God sent the Holy Spirit so we can have a fighting chance against Satan. In John 15:9–11 Jesus says, "I have loved you even as the Father has loved me. Remain in my love. When you obey my commandments, you remain in my love, just as I obey my Father's commandments and remain in his love. I have told you these things so that you will be filled with my joy. Yes, your joy will overflow!" Do you feel the passion when Jesus says, "I loved you as the Father loved me?" Do you obey His commandments so you can remain in His love? If so, you should be overflowing with His joy. If not, why not? First John 2:26–27 says, "I am writing these things to warn you about those who want to lead you astray. But you have received the Holy Spirit, and he lives within you, so you don't need anyone to teach you what is true. For the Spirit teaches you everything you need to know, and what he teaches is true—it is not a lie. So just as he has taught you, remain in fellowship with Christ."

The world is full of those who want to lead us astray. This is the importance of remaining in fellowship with Christ and acknowledging the Holy Spirit, so we can be taught everything we need to know. We need to listen to the prompting of the Spirit. The Spirit will help us to better understand and apply the Word of God to our life. He will help us grow in faith. He will lead us to church pews and fellowship with other believers. He will lead us to wherever we need to be to receive more teaching and understanding. The Spirit will lead. We must be willing to follow.

The Word of God is clear. Each of us, no matter our origin, has the opportunity to follow Christ. In Ephesians 1:13–14 Paul tells us, "And now you Gentiles have also heard the truth, the Good News that God saves you. And when you believed in Christ, he identified you as his own by giving you the Holy Spirit, whom he promised long ago. The Spirit is God's guarantee that he will give us the inheritance he promised and that he has purchased us to be his own people. He did this so we would praise and glorify him." Simply put, if you're not Jew, you're Gentile. Paul is declaring that no matter if Jew or Gentile, anyone who believes the Truth can be saved. By believing in Jesus Christ, you are identified as His own, and you are given the Holy Spirit.

The Holy Spirit is God's promise of inheriting spiritual life eternal. God fulfilled that promise when He was sacrificed on the cross, and was resurrected. Romans 8:1–5 says, "So now there is no condemnation for those who belong to Christ Jesus. And because you belong to him, the power of the life-giving Spirit has freed you from the power of sin that leads to death. The Law of Moses was unable to save us because of the weakness of our sinful nature. So God did what the law could not do. He sent his own Son in a body like the bodies we sinners have. And in that body God declared an end to sin's control over us by giving his Son as a sacrifice for our sins. He did this so that the just requirement of the law would be fully satisfied for us, who no longer follow our sinful nature but instead follow the Spirit. Those who are dominated by the sinful nature think about sinful things, but those who are controlled by the Holy Spirit think about things that please the Spirit." Paul is clearly teaching, that by belonging to Christ we are saved, we have the power of the life-giving Spirit within each of us, and sin can no longer control us. We just need to give the control over to the Spirit of God.

The Holy Spirit is our advocate and will never leave us. He will lead us to Truth. He will teach us what needs to be said, and when Satan spiritually attacks, He will provide the strength we need to be successful in spiritual battle. So if we have the strength of the Holy Spirit living in us, then why is the devil so successful at influencing us? How does he defeat us in spiritual battle? Satan is the master manipulator, and he will convince you to believe that you're not in control. But the Truth is, unless you give up control, you are in control. In his attempt to gain control, Satan will tempt you with earthly desires. This is why we need to find strength through the Spirit to rise above the temptations. We need to live less in the flesh, and more in the Spirit.

Although we know the devil has weapons and is always on the attack, we also know we have the ability to defend ourselves. So how on earth does the devil do it? How does he successfully influence our thoughts that ultimately affect our action? He is successful because we lack faith, which makes us weak in Spirit, and vulnerable to his attacks. Our spiritual strength is found in our faith. Our faith gives us the strength to trust God. Our trust in God allows us to depend on Him. Our dependence on God comes from our need for Him. Unfortunately, our need for God is most evident when we're at our lowest mentally and physically. When the devil's attacks are successful, it results in mental or physical decline. The mental and physical decline is evidenced by the continued sin in our lives and our inability to make godly choices. Because we are living in the flesh, predisposed to follow our sinful nature, and vulnerable to the attacks of Satan, we can expect to receive our fair share of war wounds and battle scars.

8

War Wounds and Battle Scars

When we think of war wounds and battle scars, what usually comes to mind is the physical and emotional cost of freedom our soldiers pay when engaged in physical warfare. But there is also a physical and emotional cost of freedom associated with spiritual warfare. When we are spiritually attacked, if we fail to obey God, and give in to our sinful nature, there will be physical and emotional wounding. But here's the major difference between physical and spiritual warfare. In physical warfare, we're not all soldiers on the frontline of attack in physical battle. In spiritual warfare, we're all soldiers on the frontline of attack in spiritual battle.

Galatians 5:17 says, "The sinful nature wants to do evil, which is just the opposite of what the Spirit wants. And the Spirit gives us desires that are the opposite of what the sinful nature desires. These two forces are constantly fighting each other, so you are not free to carry out your good intentions." Spiritual warfare is about fighting for the freedom to carry out our good intentions. Galatians

5:19–26 says, "When you follow the desires of your sinful nature, the results are very clear: sexual immorality, impurity, lustful pleasures, idolatry, sorcery, hostility, quarreling, jealousy, outbursts of anger, selfish ambition, dissension, division, envy, drunkenness, wild parties, and other sins like these. Let me tell you again, as I have before, that anyone living that sort of life will not inherit the Kingdom of God. But the Holy Spirit produces this kind of fruit in our lives: love, joy, peace, patience, kindness, goodness, faithfulness, gentleness, and self-control. There is no law against these things! Those who belong to Christ Jesus have nailed the passions and desires of their sinful nature to his cross and crucified them there. Since we are living by the Spirit, let us follow the Spirit's leading in every part of our lives. Let us not become conceited, or provoke one another, or be jealous of one another."

Go back and review the results of following the desires of our sinful nature, and Satan's lead. Now, review the results when we don't follow the desires of our sinful nature, and instead follow the Spirit's lead. When considering the spiritual condition of the world, whose lead are we following? Considering the spiritual condition of your life, whose lead are you following? If you're not sure what the answer is, then consider this. Is your sinful nature and evil ways being camouflaged and concealed by what has become the accepted and normal behavior of the world today?

Spiritual war wounds are often self-inflicted when we follow the desires of our sinful nature and Satan's lead. We can find ourselves immersed in behavior that is spiritually and physically unhealthy. The behavior can become addictive. The results are physical and emotional wounding caused by sinful choices associated with eating, smoking, alcohol, drugs, and sex. This physical and emotional wounding can easily be seen by simply looking around. It literally looks like a battlefield.

Although Satan can influence our decisions resulting in physical sickness and suffering, we are ultimately responsible for every choice we make. Then, because of our spiritual weakness, and the reality of what we've done to ourselves, it causes emotional wounding. We get depressed, and Satan is there to take us as deep and as dark as we allow. There is also self-inflicted wounding associated with sexual behavior. When we choose to be sexually promiscuous, there can be both physical and emotional wounding that can last a lifetime. Physically, we can contract sexual diseases. Emotionally, there's guilt and shame.

All the physical and emotional evidence indicates we are losing in spiritual warfare, but there's Good News. It's never too late. At any time, we have the freedom to stop following our sinful desires and Satan's lead. We can start following the Spirit's lead. We can learn to rely on the Holy Spirit for the spiritual strength we need. As a starting point, declare or restate you accept Christ as your personal Savior. Then, nail the desires of your sinful nature to the cross. After you do this, there could be times you will lose control. When you do, remember to immediately take the control back in the name of Christ. Once you regain control, you may lose it again. It's a constant battle. Keep fighting because God will provide the strength you need to ultimately be successful.

Unfortunately, spiritual war wounds are also inflicted by others. Physical and emotional wounding occurs when family members, friends, acquaintances, or complete strangers, choose to follow their sinful nature and Satan's lead. The results can be gut wrenching and devastating. We see it by how much wounding is associated with the abuse of women, children, and the elderly. We see it by how much wounding is associated with pornography, prostitution, human trafficking, rape, and child molestation. We see it by how much wounding is associated with bullying and cyberbullying. We see it by how much wounding is associated with the hateful and violent response to a person's religion, race, color, national origin, gender, sexual orientation, or political affiliation. As soldiers on the frontline in spiritual battle, we should be rallying to combat sexual immorality, impurity, lustful pleasures, hostility, quarreling, anger, selfish ambition, dissension, and division. Why do we accept what we see in the world today as the new normal? Is there anything normal about it?

There are many depths and complexities to spiritual war wounds. Some wounding can seem so subtle and insignificant at the time, we don't give it much thought. But here's the problem. If these wounds aren't properly dealt with, they won't heal. They can fester into wounds that never heal, and the pain can last a lifetime. There is also wounding that is so devastating at the time it is inflicted, it can be hard to imagine getting through the pain and suffering. Unfortunately, because we let our guard down, the most hurtful wounding can come from those we love and trust the most. We can be taken advantage of because we're young, innocent, or naïve. When wounded by those we love and trust, we often try to justify their actions by finding fault in ourselves. Ironically, many who have been wounded by the ones they love and trust use it as an excuse to justify their actions when wounding the ones they love. Some inner circles can perpetuate a seemingly never-ending cycle of wounding. If this sinful behavior continues to go unchecked, it can escalate into years of physical and emotional wounding. But there's more Good News. The cycle of wounding can be broken. Through the strength of the Holy Spirit, and the promise of Jesus Christ, we can find peace through the grace and forgiveness of God.

Battle scars are formed when the physical and emotional war wounds of spiritual warfare heal. The indication of whether a wound has truly healed is found in on our ability to forgive ourselves, or others. In Matthew 6:14–15 Jesus says, "If you forgive those who sin against you, your heavenly Father will forgive you. But if you refuse to forgive others, your Father will not forgive your sins." Luke 6:37 says, "Do not judge others, and you will not be judged. Do not condemn others, or it will all come back against you. Forgive others and you will be forgiven." We are all sinners. We all need forgiveness. But to forgive, does not mean to forget. Although we may never forget, we must forgive. We must give it to God and trust Him. But here's a caution for the memories you can't forget. Satan will use the emotions associated with past wounding to spiritually attack you in the present. He'll reopen healed wounds in an effort to continue to cause as much pain and suffering as possible. To combat this, we must keep pursuing an ongoing relationship with Jesus Christ. He provides the strength we need through the Spirit, to truly forgive and find peace.

When you give thought to your spiritual battle scars, what comes to mind? Do you see yourself covered with ugly scars of shame? Our battle scars are nothing to be ashamed of. Matter of fact, they are a beautiful reflection of God's grace. It's our choice to live in disgrace, or live in His grace. It's our choice to allow the negativity and the darkness of our past to affect and define our future. We can make the choice to walk in the Light and the peace of knowing we are loved by God. God uses every one of our war wounds and battle scars to help us spiritually transform into who He wants us to be. If we let our past define us, Satan will use everything we've been through to take even more advantage of us. If we let God use our past to refine us, He will use everything we've been through to make us spiritually stronger, and Satan will no longer be able to take advantage of us. This is why so many wounded and broken people give such great testimonies. When we rise above the circumstances of our wounding, it gives witness to God's strength and peace in our lives. It gives hope to those still suffering. It lets them know they are not alone in their suffering. This hope is a part of furthering the Kingdom of God.

Do you ever find yourself questioning why God allows all the suffering? Some will watch their innocent children suffer with sickness and disease. Some children will suffer the consequences of medical procedures and treatments, and some will die at a young age. Some children will be taken advantage of, or abused. We hope and pray, but can't help wondering, why doesn't God intervene? Why would God allow the innocent children to suffer? There are also adults who suffer with sickness and disease. From our viewpoint, whether young or old, too many people die an untimely death that doesn't seem fair. Some people will have accidents that can cause pain and suffering that lasts a lifetime. Some accidents kill in an instant. Sometimes life unfolds in a way that just doesn't make any sense at all. Then, when we add a loving God into the equation, it becomes even more confusing. How does a loving God know and not intervene?

To help us understand, it's important to be reminded of our history. In the beginning, we were innocent and free of sin. God warned the first man not to eat from the tree of the knowledge of good and evil. Genesis 2:16–17 says, "But the Lord God warned him, 'You may freely eat the fruit of every tree in the garden—except the tree of the knowledge of good and evil. If you eat the fruit, you are sure to die.'" Realizing man needed a helper just right for him, God created woman. Both man and woman lived in the garden and were enjoying a personal relationship with God, until Satan successfully influenced the woman to eat the fruit from the forbidden tree. Genesis 3:4-7 says, "'You won't die!' the serpent replied to the woman. 'God knows that your eyes will be opened as soon as you eat it, and you will be like God, knowing both good and evil.' The woman was convinced. She saw that the tree was beautiful and its fruit looked delicious, and she wanted the wisdom it would give her. So she took some of the fruit and ate it. Then she gave some to her husband, who was with her, and he ate it, too. At that moment their eyes were opened, and they suddenly felt shame at their nakedness. So they sewed fig leaves together to cover themselves." Because of their disobedience, they both gained the knowledge of good and evil, and were banished from the garden.

Fast forward, and here we are today. Satan is still using our sinful nature and our refusal to obey God against us. But now, instead of it involving two people in a garden, it involves a fallen world. We must stop blaming God. Even though we live in a fallen world with so much pain and suffering, we still continue to follow our sinful nature and Satan's lead, instead of following the Spirit's lead. God, knowing there is no hope of rising above the despair on our own; He sent His one and only Son to save us. He also sent the Holy Spirit to help us, comfort us, and guide us through this life. Thanks to the Father's love and mercy, we have renewed hope in knowing we can have abundant life here on Earth, and we can look forward to spiritual life eternal.

Although God doesn't always take our pain away, He knows our needs, and He hears our prayers. So why doesn't He just answer them? Think about it, if every prayer was answered immediately upon request, it would eliminate the need for faith. If we received immediate healing for all our aches and pain, we would take the answers to prayers for granted. God knows what's best for us at all times. Although we might think we really need something, God gives us what we need, when we need it. God is the creator, omnipotent or all powerful, omniscient or all-knowing. God is dealing with things we can't see, or imagine. He's working in a timeframe of eternity. Although we may say we believe in this ultimate destination called heaven, how often do we stop to consider the reality of eternity? If eternity is promised, shouldn't we be focusing more of our time on spiritually preparing for it?

One of the reasons God allows us to experience pain and suffering, is to keep us mindful that it was our sin that caused Christ to endure such pain and suffering. Christ suffered not because He deserved it, but because we deserve it. If God were to take away all our pain and suffering associated with living in this fallen world, would we take Him for granted? Sure we would. Even knowing He sent His Son to shed His blood to pay for our sin, we still take Him for granted. God allows suffering because it leads us to depend on Him. Think about it, when do we tend to reach out to God? Is it when our lives are going great and we're as happy as can be? Or is it when our lives aren't going so well?

How many times have you reached out to God and promised Him, if He'll just give you this, or get you through that, you'll never ask for anything again? How many times have you reached out and promised God, if He'll heal you this one time, you'll never take another day for granted? We mean it at the time, with all our heart and soul, but how many of us break our promises? The Good News is, even though we break our promises, God never breaks His. Even though we take Him for granted, He never gives up on us. If we can admit we take God for granted, then we have to admit, our pain and suffering keeps us dependent on Him.

Our pain and suffering reminds us of who we are, and what we did. It reminds us of the pain and suffering endured by our Savior, Jesus Christ, to save us. The image of Jesus hanging on the cross is the inspiration we need to be thankful, regardless of our circumstances. First Thessalonians 5:18 says, "Be thankful in all circumstances, for this is God's will for you who belong to Christ Jesus." Romans 8:16–18 says, "For his Spirit joins with our spirit to affirm that we are God's children. And since we are his children, we are his heirs. In fact, together with Christ we are heirs of God's glory. But if we are to share his glory, we must also share his suffering. Yet what we suffer now is nothing compared to the glory he will reveal to us later." What a promise, right?

Our dependence on God, our relationship with Christ, and our thankful heart, provides the opportunity to show our family, our friends, our neighbors, and the world, there is so much more to us than what meets the eye. When we rise above adversity, pain and suffering, our resolve and strength causes those observing to wonder how we can maintain such a positive attitude, when everything seems to be going so wrong. Our example of being positive and thankful at all times is our opportunity to shine the Light of hope in Jesus Christ. When people observe us, they should see our strength of Spirit and our peace in Christ. What they shouldn't see is our spiritual war wounds and battle scars. Our past does not define us. Our past refines us into something beautiful, something Godly, and something spiritual. Spirituality is a refining process. We should never stop spiritually transforming into a better version of ourselves. If we become complacent, and think we have reached our highest level of spiritual transformation, the enemy is whispering to us. If we stop spiritually transforming, Satan will use our complacency to spiritually attack us. He wants to influence us to move away from the Light, and back toward the darkness.

Christ's suffering was not just a physical sacrifice, it was a spiritual victory. Jesus provided living proof, that death in the flesh is not the end. Just as He conquered the grave, we too can look forward to spiritual victory. We can have eternal life with a loving God, through Jesus Christ. Life in the flesh is but a speck of time in comparison to eternity.

We may never understand every circumstance or situation we find ourselves in. We can't always rationalize everything we have to go through. But our lack of answers should inspire us to pursue more biblical knowledge. The more knowledge we acquire, the more we understand who God is, the more faith we will have.

9

Faith

Faith is at the very core of Christianity. The word faith is synonymous with belief and trust. Hebrews 11:1–3 says, "Faith shows the reality of what we hope for; it is the evidence of things we cannot see. Through their faith, the people in days of old earned a good reputation. By faith we understand that the entire universe was formed at God's command, that what we now see did not come from anything that can be seen." Faith requires we step out of our comfort zone to believe in something we can't fully see or understand. Ironically, because of our God-given ability to acquire knowledge, we think we should be able to figure everything out. The mind literally gets in the way of faith because Satan uses the thought processes to spiritually attack, causing us to have doubt and question our faith.

Faith doesn't come easy. It's a work in progress. It requires we not only read God's Word, but study His Word to increase knowledge. Because His Truth is timeless, His teachings and principles are as relevant today as when originally written. As we develop a better understanding of the Truth, it will profoundly affect our faith by providing insight into everything from creation to eternal life. Without reading and studying the Word of God, we can't possibly understand the complexity of God. Even with His Word we struggle because we lack faith. Hebrews 11:6 says, "And it is impossible to please God without faith. Anyone who wants to come to him must believe that God exists and that he rewards those who sincerely seek him." In Matthew 7:7 Jesus says, "Keep on asking and you will receive what you ask for. Keep on seeking, and you will find. Keep on knocking, and the door will be opened for you." Do you have the faith to keep asking, seeking, and knocking?

Faith also requires we dedicate the time to pursue a personal relationship with God. The closer our relationship with Christ, the more faith and confidence we'll have to surrender to the Spirit. Life dependent upon the Spirit enables us to live less of an existence in the flesh, and more of a spiritual existence. The more we embrace our spirituality, the more we can experience God's love. Attending church is a wonderful way to enhance our personal relationship with God, by motivating us to pursue a deeper, more meaningful and loving relationship with Him. The church does this by providing insight into God's Word, and guidance on how to apply His Word to how we live. Although the importance of the church cannot be overstated, it doesn't replace the need for us to personally pursue God. The personal effort we put into seeking God impacts the depth of our personal relationship with Him. Our personal walk with Christ directly impacts our ability to feel the Spirit, which increases faith.

Our faith is challenged by the trials and tribulations we encounter. We lose faith because we have difficulty understanding why things go horribly wrong. But ironically, we always seem to have just enough faith to blame or cuss God. When we are weak in faith, the devil uses the opportunity to shoot those fiery arrows of doubt. Then, while in a state of self-pity and doubt, just as quickly as things went horribly wrong, they go wonderfully right, and we regain our faith. When things are going wonderfully right, do we take the opportunity to praise and thank God as quickly as we blamed or cussed God for our troubles? Life can feel like a rollercoaster ride. At times it can be very scary, at other times it can be fun. When we get scared it's very important to not lose faith. We must keep the faith to remain spiritually strong. It helps us rise above adversity by knowing in our heart, better times will come.

There's more to faith than just believing in Jesus Christ. Faith requires we believe in the Trinity which includes the Father, the Son, and the Holy Spirit. All three are God and an important part of faith. Faith requires we believe in God the Father, the omnipotent (all-powerful, almighty), omniscient (all-knowing and all-seeing) creator. Faith requires we believe in Jesus Christ, God the Son, the Savior, sent by the Father to walk with us, talk with us, teach us, and ultimately die for us. Faith requires we believe in the Holy Spirit, sent by the Father to guide, comfort, and help us understand all things spiritual. Faith in all three brings about a spiritual transformation that will profoundly change your heart and life.

God created us for relationship, and He has always made the effort to interact with us. Some heard His voice, and many witnessed His miracles. He used dreams and visions to speak through prophets. He commanded life-altering events and miracles to materialize to fulfill His ultimate plan. As part of God's perfect plan, the Son of God was born of a virgin, and while with us, Jesus performed miracles to be witnessed. He commanded the demons to be gone, the lame to walk, and the blind to see. He healed the sick, and raised the dead. He taught the Word of God like no other. In an incredible act of love, Christ fulfilled the Father's plan by becoming the ultimate and final sacrifice on the cross for our sin. John 19:30 says, "When Jesus had tasted it, he said, 'It is finished!' Then he bowed his head and gave up his spirit." God has done everything in His power for us to know the Truth. It's now up to us to have the faith to believe the Truth.

We struggle with faith because we have difficulty understanding God's love. How can God love us? We're not worthy. The Truth is we're not worthy. But we are made worthy through our faith in Jesus Christ. Romans 3:21–26 says, "But now God has shown us a way to be made right with him without keeping the requirement of the law, as was promised in the writings of Moses and the prophets long ago. We are made right with God by placing our faith in Jesus Christ. And this is true for everyone who believes, no matter who we are. For everyone has sinned; we all fall short of God's glorious standard. Yet God, in his grace, freely makes us right in his sight. He did this through Christ Jesus when he freed us from the penalty of our sins. For God presented Jesus as the sacrifice for sin. People are made right with God when they believe that Jesus sacrificed his life, shedding his blood. This sacrifice shows that God was being fair when he held back and did not punish those who sinned in times past, for he was looking ahead and including them in what he would do in this present time. God did this to demonstrate his righteousness, for he himself is fair and just, and he makes sinners right in his sight when they believe in Jesus." Through the shed blood of Christ, we have an opportunity for a restored relationship with the Father. Guiltlessness and righteousness are received through faith, and the Holy Spirit confirms our sins are forgiven.

Faith requires we believe that all the miraculous events documented in the Bible are true and actually happened. Our faith gets tested because it requires we believe in things we did not see for ourselves. Then, because God blessed us with the ability to think, analyze, deduct, and retain information, we become intellectually prideful. The devil will use our pride to create doubt in our mind. He'll influence us into thinking, if we didn't see it, or we can't make sense of it, then it can't be true. Because we didn't actually see creation, Satan will influence us to believe in theories like the big bang. Because we didn't actually see God breathe the first man into existence, and then create the first woman from the rib of man, Satan will influence us to believe in nothing but evolution. Satan will influence us to question everything biblical. He especially does not want us to believe Jesus was sacrificed on the cross to pay for our sins.

When we look at everything we do get to see, it's important to our faith, that we acknowledge God in everything. We do get to see how the Earth rotates on its axis in perfect agreement with the sun, the moon, and the entire solar system. We do get to see a star-filled sky that gives us pause to marvel in awe of it all. We do get to see the oceans brimming with sea life beyond imagination, with a massive shoreline kept at bay. We do get to see the mountain ranges so majestically formed, yet so visually peaceful. We do get to see plants and animals with beauty and function beyond comprehension. Our ability to see all creation should remind us of who we are in comparison to who God is. We are the created, He is the creator.

If we want to further strengthen our faith, we must acknowledge God in how we have survived, multiplied, and evolved, since the beginning. Not only do we continue to survive, but thanks to our God-given ability to make life-changing discoveries, we are blessed with comforts, many take for granted. We get to enjoy the daily comforts of air conditioning and heating. With a flick of a switch, *let there be light*. There's food available by stopping at a grocery store, or restaurant. With the simple turn of a faucet, we are blessed with running water. What blessings, right? There are a lot of people who don't get to enjoy all the comforts others do, but overall, as a human race, we have evolved beyond what we thought possible. But nothing is impossible with God.

Of all God's provisions, one of the most important is His Word. He provided His Word to teach us what was, what is, and what is to come. It provides every teaching necessary to successfully live life abundant. It reminds us of the promise of life eternal. It provides the knowledge we need to understand who God is, and who we are in the creation order. It teaches us how to have a personal relationship with God the Father, through Jesus Christ the Son. God's Word confirms, by believing in Christ, we are filled with the Holy Spirit. John 7:38–39 says, "Anyone who believes in me may come and drink! For the Scriptures declare, 'Rivers of living water will flow from his heart.' (When he said "living water," he was speaking of the Spirit, who would be given to everyone believing in him. But the Spirit had not yet been given, because Jesus had not yet entered into his glory.)" The Word of God deepens our faith. God knowing our every need graciously provided us with a record of historical events that has been passed down from generation to generation. The Bible's survival, and its revision by scholars to help us better understand God, is a testament that God is in control.

The Bible is as relevant today as it was when written. God never changes, and He is the constant Truth in our lives. Hebrews 13:8 says, "Jesus Christ is the same yesterday, today, and forever." Malachi 3:6 says, "I am the Lord, and I do not change." Isaiah 40:8 says, "The grass withers and the flowers fade, but the word of our God stands forever." It is crucial that we never underestimate the importance of understanding why the Bible was written and what it teaches. The written Word provides the Truth and knowledge we need to truly believe, deeply trust, and further develop faith. We must have the faith to believe that everything we see, everything we feel, and everything we experience, involves a loving God.

In a world so overrun by evil and corruption, we can easily find ourselves losing faith and trust in mankind. Consequently, it causes us to lose faith and trust in God.

This lack of faith leaves us more vulnerable to the spiritual attacks of Satan, and we become a part of the evil and corruption. Our only hope of rising above our circumstances is to develop the faith to turn back to God. We must learn to rely on the strength of the Spirit to be more successful in battling Satan and finding true peace. Although we will still face daily challenges, the stress will no longer dominate our mind. We'll have the faith to trust that everything will work out according to God's plan. Take a moment to pause right now and look back on your life. Identify the times, even though you weren't being faithful, trusting, or dependent on God, He had you anyway. God truly is in all things, at all times, according to His plan.

So what keeps you from taking a leap of faith? What keeps you from accepting and receiving God's love, grace, forgiveness, and the peace that comes when you have the faith to trust Him? I challenge you to take a leap of faith, to completely trust God, and to give the control over to Him. You can't buy or earn what God offers; it's a gift. If you think because you've fallen short your whole life, you don't have a chance, you're dead wrong. Matter of fact, the more broken you can admit you are, the more likely you are to realize how much you need God. To begin experiencing a relationship with God, declare you accept His gift of grace and forgiveness. Ephesians 2:8–10 says, "God saved you by his grace when you believed. And you can't take credit for this; it is a gift from God. Salvation is not a reward for the good things we have done, so none of us can boast about it. For we are God's masterpiece. He has created us anew in Christ Jesus, so we can do the good things he planned for us long ago." Don't you want to be a part of the good things God planned for you? Taking a leap of faith can be very challenging. It requires we do things we're not used to. It requires we give up control of our life. Instead of doing everything our way, we need to do it His Way. His Way requires we do better at obeying the Word of God. It requires we do better at following the Spirit's lead, instead of following our sinful desires and Satan's influences.

So go ahead, take a leap of faith and watch what happens. What do you have to lose? What do you have to gain? You would gain the opportunity to experience a loving relationship with God. More importantly, you would gain the opportunity to have all your relationships impacted by the same grace and forgiveness God freely offers you.

10
Grace and Forgiveness

Although none of us deserve it, because He loves us, God offers His grace and forgiveness. Through the shed blood of Jesus Christ, God's grace offers the opportunity to be forgiven, free from the guilt and shame of our sins. Ephesians 2:8 says, "God saved you by his grace when you believed. And you can't take credit for this; it is a gift from God." Matthew 6:14–15 says, "If you forgive those who sin against you, your heavenly Father will forgive you. But if you refuse to forgive others, your Father will not forgive your sins." After what God did for us, can we justify withholding grace and forgiveness from another? Can we justify withholding it from ourselves? Withholding grace and forgiveness does not come from the Spirit of God; it comes from the influence of Satan. Satan is the opposite of love, he is hate, and he's all about severed relationships. He wants us to judge one another. He wants us to judge ourselves.

Isn't it interesting how quick we are to so harshly judge and then hold a grudge? Don't we all know people, friends, and families, who hold grudges? Some last a lifetime. If we profess to be followers of Christ, what kind of an example is this for those looking on? Does it tell a story of a loving and caring God? Does it shine Light into the darkness?

By withholding grace and forgiveness, we are not following the example of our Savior, and we are not obeying what God tells us to do. Colossians 3:13–14 says, "Make allowances for each other's faults, and forgive anyone who offends you. Remember, the Lord forgave you, so you must forgive others. Above all, clothe yourselves with love, which binds us all together in perfect harmony." We must humble ourselves by remembering, God allowed His one and only Son to suffer and die for our sin. Because of this unimaginable display of love, we have been given the opportunity to once again, be in a loving relationship with Him. This should spiritually inspire and motivate us to clothe ourselves in love, and offer this same grace and forgiveness to one another, and ourselves. How has our failure to offer grace and forgiveness affected our personal relationships? How many marriages founded on God's love has failed? How many relationships between family members, friends, and neighbors, have been damaged or destroyed?

God is a God of loving relationship. God's design of the family provides the foundation for loving relationships that makes us stronger individually, and collectively as a family unit. We should see the foundational love of God's design for the family in all other relationships.

We all come from the same beginning. Man was created in the image of God, then woman. God gave us the ability to procreate, and throughout time, two became four, four became eight, and so on. Although we all came from the same beginning, based on our family lineage, we evolved with different characteristics. From a physical perspective, each of us has unique skin color. None of us are generically white or black, yellow or brown. Can you imagine if we all looked alike? For that reason alone, we should be celebrating our differences.

Labeling by skin color is a lie. Satan is the Father of Lies, so who do you think is behind our ungodly obsession with skin color? Our physical differences should never be a justification for division and hate. If you find yourself judging or hating because someone doesn't look like you, do you think this represents godly behavior? What if someone doesn't dress, act, or think like you, do you find yourself judging? Our differences don't make anyone inferior or superior. Besides, who died and left you in charge? Jesus died, He's in charge.

From a mental perspective, our personality is as unique as our skin color. Can you imagine if we all acted the same? How boring. We may be different physically and mentally, but our differences enable us to see things from diverse perspectives. It not only stimulates personal growth, it makes us collectively stronger. Our world is stronger for our differences, not our similarities. We need to embrace our differences. We are created in the image of God, but it doesn't make us God. He is perfect; we're not. We all make ungodly choices, and we will continue to make mistakes, but we need to do better at approaching everyone with God's love in mind, instead of Satan's hate.

All relationships, if founded on God's love, should be relationships of love and support. Because we will always run from hate, hating someone for their personal choices pushes them away. It creates an emotional divide. Because we will always run toward love, loving someone through their personal choices pulls them in. It creates an emotional bond. We don't have to agree with every choice a loved one makes, but we do have a responsibility to love them through their choices. When we stop loving people because of their choices, it eliminates the hope of having a godly influence on their lives.

How many relationships are severed because someone is not willing to tolerate another's personal choice? How many mothers and daughters, fathers and sons, siblings, family members, friends, and neighbors, have lost loving relationships because of their refusal to offer grace and forgiveness? Why are we so quick to throw love away and replace it with hate? Severed relationships are the result of appointing ourselves judge and jury. When we judge others, what standard are we using? As we look at our own lives, should we be judging others? Is it sinful pride and arrogance? Do we forget we are all sinners, none worthy of God's love? In Matthew 7:1–2 Jesus says, "Do not judge others, and you will not be judged. For you will be treated as you treat others. The standard you use in judging is the standard by which you will be judged." How plain and simple is this to understand? This should make us think long and hard about how we judge and treat one another, and how we withhold grace and forgiveness. Do you want to be judged as harshly as you judge? Or do you want the grace and forgiveness God offers? You can't have it both ways.

Emotions associated with hate, leads to a life of bitterness and resentment, because hateful emotions are contradictory to everything God. When we withhold love, we are sinning against God by not obeying what He commands us to do. In John 13:34–35 Jesus says, "So now I am giving you a new commandment: Love each other. Just as I have loved you, you should love each other. Your love for one another will prove to the world that you are my disciples." A *command*ment by definition is a *command*. It's not optional. When we go against what God commands, our disobedience has a negative effect on our spiritual growth and strength.

When we look at what's going on in the world, what does it give witness to? Do we see more of God's love, or Satan's hate? God's Word is perfectly clear about how we must love one another, yet it's amazing how many people try to justify withholding grace and forgiveness with the Word of God. Scripture does not contradict itself. When we withhold grace and forgiveness, we withhold love, we deny healing, we embrace bitterness, and we are giving in to what Satan wants. This is just another example of the devil's strategy to isolate us. He wants us to hold on to our hate, bitterness, and rage. He wants us to have an unforgiving spirit.

We are all guilty of hurting someone else and it's important to ask for forgiveness. But regardless of whether that person forgives you, it's important you forgive yourself. Forgiving yourself is something you control, and it affects your personal well-being. It affects you physically, emotionally, and spiritually. Although gaining someone else's forgiveness can be beneficial to the relationship, you can't force someone to forgive you. If someone withholds forgiveness, or offers it in an insincere way, they are responsible for their actions. They are accountable to God. It affects their well-being. We should never let someone else's decision to withhold forgiveness affect our personal well-being. Forgiving those who don't forgive us releases the bitterness associated with holding on to the emotion they want us to live with.

Many times, the forgiveness we offer is a shallow offering of words. It's not heartfelt and lacks positive action. Positive action is an ongoing process that indicates heartfelt sincerity. It requires we have the emotional control to not let negative thoughts and feelings creep back into the mind. When this happens, Satan is gaining a foothold. We must use the strength of the Spirit to work our mind and heart back to positive action. If the action remains negative, you have not truly forgiven. If the action remains positive, it's a good indication you have truly forgiven.

God offered His forgiveness in an unimaginable act of love. He sent His Son to be hung on a cross. He died a slow agonizing death on our behalf. He was the final sacrifice to once and for all, pay for our sin. If we are willing to accept God's grace, forgiveness, and love, why do we struggle to offer grace, forgiveness, and love to ourselves, or another? This is more proof that the enemy is winning in spiritual warfare. When we allow Satan to influence us, we believe it's our right to judge and hate, especially ourselves. We assume what we've done is much worse than what other people have done. The evil one wants us to conclude we are horrible in comparison. The truth is we have no clue what other people have done or what's been done to them. We are not to compare ourselves to others to validate our self-worth. We are to validate our self-worth through Christ and His love for us.

How much does God love us? He came down from the spiritual realm, knowing He would die an agonizing death for our sin. He came to teach us, and by example, show us how to live. After dying He was raised from the dead, He ascended back to the spiritual realm, and the Holy Spirit descended to help us, and Christ is sitting in the place of honor at God's right hand, pleading for us. Thanks to Christ we have the opportunity to once again be in right standing with God. So again, how much does God love us? Ephesians 3:18–19 says, "And may you have the power to understand, as all God's people should, how wide, how long, how high, and how deep his love is. May you experience the love of Christ, though it is too great to understand fully. Then you will be made complete with all the fullness of life and power that comes from God."

To fully experience and understand the love of Christ, we must be able to communicate with Him. Although we can talk to Him, at times, we need the communication to be reverent. After all, He is God. We need to learn to go to Him in respectful prayer.

11
Prayer

One of the most important parts of any relationship is honest communication. It allows insight into who we truly are. As we learn to trust someone, we begin to divulge more of our innermost thoughts. This allows the relationship the potential of developing into a more meaningful, caring, and loving relationship. Our relationship with God is similar, but there's an obvious difference, He is God. He's omniscient or all-knowing, so He already knows us to the core. He knows our true heart. So instead of a relationship where we're both getting to know each other, it's more about us getting to know Him. What's really interesting is, the better we know Him, the better we know ourselves.

Our relationship with God also requires honest communication. The more honest we are with Him, the more honest we will be with ourselves. We must learn to trust God with our innermost thoughts. This can be a concern for many, but remember, He is God and He already knows us intimately. So if you want to develop a more meaningful, loving, and caring relationship with Him, be honest, be real, be you. Don't try to be something you're not. You're only fooling yourself.

When we think, God knows what we're thinking. When we talk, God knows what we're saying. When we pray, God knows what we're praying. Although all three are wonderful ways to communicate with God, prayer is another one of His provisions. It's the most respectful, reverent, heartfelt, honest, and spiritually stimulating way to communicate with Him. It's an important feature of being in a personal relationship with God. Ephesians 6:18 says, "Pray in the Spirit at all times and on every occasion. Stay alert and be persistent in your prayers for all believers everywhere."

When the Word teaches us to pray at all times and on every occasion, it doesn't leave much to interpretation. We need to pray every day, and we need to pray in the Spirit. It strengthens our relationship with God, because through the Spirit, we hear God. During prayer, we need to be silent and alert to identify those spiritually stimulating times to hear and feel the Spirit. In John 16:15 Jesus says, "The Spirit will tell you whatever he receives from me." Prayer is a spiritual experience that keeps us spiritually connected. It improves our communication with God. It lets the Spirit feel our heart, which in turn, allows us to feel the Spirit.

In Matthew 6:7 Jesus says, "When you pray, don't babble on and on as the Gentiles do. They think their prayers are answered merely by repeating their words again and again." In other words, don't memorize and repeat emotionally empty words when you pray. Instead, pray to God with an emotionally sincere heart. Pray to Him with the love, affection, and adoration He deserves.

When praying, don't be surprised when you lose focus and your mind wanders. You'll find yourself thinking about things not even related to what you were praying about. When this happens, Satan is on the attack, because he knows you're connecting with the Spirit, and he wants to distract you. When this happens, in the name of Jesus Christ, take the control back. Pick up where you left off, and smile, because you know who's really in control, and so does Satan.

Regardless of whether our prayers are answered or not, we must give thanks to the Lord for everything He has done, everything He is doing, and everything He will do in the future. Having a thankful Spirit makes it difficult to have a complaining spirit. A thankful Spirit results in a positive attitude. It helps us to shine the Light into the darkness, by allowing those observing, to witness something different in the way we live our lives. Our Light should spark those in the darkness to wonder why, regardless of the circumstances, we always seem so joyful and at peace.

Because tomorrow isn't promised, don't take any day for granted. Start every new day prayerfully thanking God for the opportunity. Let Him know how you're looking forward to what the new day will bring. As you pray, keep mindful of God's power, God's love, and God's grace. Ask Him for forgiveness where you fail Him. It's powerful to end all prayer in the name of Jesus Christ. The more sincere, personal, and heartfelt the prayer, the more likely you will be in agreement with the Spirit, and the will of God. This keeps you focused on what's most important, because your will is not always in agreement with the will of God.

Don't be discouraged when you don't get what you pray for. Just because you want something, doesn't mean you'll get it. Your desires can be in conflict with God's will. It's about His timing, not yours. James 4:3 says, "And even when you ask, you don't get it because your motives are all wrong—you want only what will give you pleasure." God knows what's best for you. You must trust Him, give the control to Him, and have the faith to believe He'll give you what you need, when you need it. You must be patient, because His timing is perfect. Psalm 27:14 says, "Wait patiently for the Lord. Be brave and courageous. Yes, wait patiently for the Lord."

When it comes to what you want and when you want it, how patient are you? Our foresight can be very blurry, because we lack the clarity to know what to do in every situation. But our hindsight is always clear. We can look back on our decisions and clearly see what the right choice was, and what we should have done differently. God's foresight is never blurry, it's perfectly clear. He is perfect, so therefore, His vision and plans for us are perfect. God's perfect vision directly impacts our imperfect prayer life. It determines the outcome of prayer. This is where our faith and trust in God are rooted. It's how we experience God's peace, no matter the circumstances.

Unanswered prayers can be blessings in disguise. Look back on your life and recall the times you prayed for something, and your prayers weren't answered. At the time, what you thought was a setback, over time, proved to be a blessing. Maybe you didn't get a job or promotion, but as a result, something better happened. Or you came to realize, that particular job wasn't right for you. Was it possible God was answering someone else's prayer at the time? Now that's hard to imagine. At the same time you're praying for a job, somebody else is praying for the same job.

How about the relationships you prayed for that didn't work out? Then, over time, you realized you were just settling, or were afraid of being alone. Maybe you didn't realize how unhappy you were until you got out of the relationship. Later you ended up in a better relationship, and found true happiness. Take time right now to look back on your life to identify the times when your will clearly conflicted with the will of God. Even though you might not have been happy at the time, thank God for what He did. If we learn from each experience, we can learn to trust God. In future relationships, we can have the faith to give the control to Him. Believing that God truly knows what's best for us will help us get through the challenging relationships without being so unhappy and miserable.

If we examine God's track record compared to ours, who should we be depending on? He created us, He saved us, and He provides for us. He is involved with every aspect of our life. If you believe that God is in everything, this should truly "wow" you. Let God put the "wow" in your life by trusting Him with all aspects of your life. Thank Him for everything He provides. When the time comes and you don't agree with God, or don't understand what He's doing, give Him the benefit of the doubt. Have the faith to trust Him, and give Him the final control. He is God, so let God be God.

It's very important to spend some of our prayer time without distraction. Devote time to quietly be with God. Respect God by giving Him your full and undivided attention. Find a place that feels peaceful and comfortable. Start praying and allow five minutes. Set a timer if necessary. As you get more into it, you'll be amazed at how fast five minutes goes by. Add more time. Eventually you won't need a timer. You'll find yourself comfortable in prayer, and using the perfect amount of time that feels just right.

Your prayer life will profoundly influence your personal relationship with God. It will help you gain insight and understanding into who He is, and what He has planned for you. As you devote more time to prayer, you will experience a stirring of the Spirit that conveys all is well. Some people say they have never felt or heard the Spirit of God. How much time are they spending with Him? Although most people really do want to hear and feel the Spirit of God, most don't devote enough time. How much time did you devote to God last week? Last month?

Our personal and private prayer life is an important component of our spiritual growth and development, but it's also important to pray in public. We should be willing to embrace every opportunity to pray out loud. It conveys an important message to those looking on. It says we are willing to acknowledge God in public. In Matthew 10:32 Jesus says, "Everyone who acknowledges me publicly here on earth, I will also acknowledge before my Father in heaven."

Some people are too shy or reluctant to pray out loud. If you're reluctant, it's most likely because you are weak in faith, and weak in Spirit. Satan will use your weakness against you. If you're shy, the devil will use your shyness against you. He'll influence you to shy away from acknowledging God in public. Satan will influence you to compare your ability to pray with the ability of others. He'll have you believing your prayers aren't good enough. Don't let Satan's fiery arrows of doubt keep you from praying. Praying out loud doesn't come easy. Most everyone is nervous at first. The more you do it, the less intimidating it is. No matter how you feel, just relax. Just be you.

Prayer shouldn't be a structured set of memorized words. It should be sincere, heartfelt, and directed at spiritually influencing the circumstances of life. Find the courage to step out in faith the first time. Each time thereafter, it will be less stressful, spiritually fulfilling, and more joyful. Depend on the strength of the Spirit to keep your mind focused. Keep prayer simple. Don't try to impress the listeners. When praying out loud, you never know who you are blessing. What a great opportunity to be a witness for Christ and a part of furthering the Kingdom of God.

Satan wants to take advantage of our spiritual weakness to separate us from God. By praying, we are embracing our unity with the Spirit of God, giving us the spiritual strength needed to battle Satan. Prayer fortifies the heart, and because the heart is the fort, it helps us mount a defense against the enemy. Because the mind is the battlefield, prayer also helps us mount an offense by including God in our thoughts and plans. Prayer lets Satan know we are in communication with a loving God. It lets him know, we are fully aware, there's nothing he can do to separate us from the love of God. Romans 8:38–39 says, "And I am convinced that nothing can ever separate us from God's love. Neither death nor life, neither angels nor demons, neither our fears for today nor our worries about tomorrow—not even the powers of hell can separate us from God's love. No power in the sky above or in the earth below—indeed, nothing in all creation will ever be able to separate us from the love of God that is revealed in Christ Jesus our Lord." This is such Good News.

You might think you're not worthy of God hearing, or answering your prayers. You are made worthy through the shed blood of Jesus Christ on the cross. When you pray, do you truly believe you are communicating with a living God? A God who died on the cross? A God who later appeared to give witness to the Truth that He indeed conquered the grave? For you to truly believe that God hears your prayers, you must truly believe He is real and He is alive.

12

God Is Real, God Is Alive

Believing in God is a process of the mind and heart. The mind involves the use of our God-given ability to comprehend and retain. It enables us to understand the Word of God, empowering us to know God. The more we know God, the more we will want to pursue Him. The heart enables us to feel the Spirit of God in us. It motivates us to want to know even more. The more knowledge we acquire, the more spiritual feelings we develop. How and what we spiritually feel, ultimately validates and confirms, God is real and God is alive.

God's Word says if you truly believe in God, then you have the Holy Spirit living in you. Romans 8:11 says, "The Spirit of God, who raised Jesus from the dead, lives in you. And just as God raised Christ Jesus from the dead, he will give life to your mortal bodies by this same Spirit living within you." Second Timothy 1:14 says, "Through the power of the Holy Spirit who lives within us, carefully guard the precious truth that has been entrusted to you." The presence of the Holy Spirit is living proof, God is alive.

Although God made His Word available so we can know the Truth, even with the Truth we struggle. We struggle because God loves us in a way that can't be fully understood from a human perspective. Then, because of our sinful nature and prideful demeanor, we embrace more of what we think, and less of what we spiritually feel. The chasm between what we think and how we feel is where Satan spiritually attacks. He wants to keep us from experiencing God. The Good News is, even though we struggle with spirituality and loving God, He never struggles with loving us. God is love, so regardless of how we pursue or love Him, He never stops pursuing or loving us. This is why we all find God at different times in our lives. We find Him when we listen to the prompting of the Spirit and follow our heart, because when we decide to pursue God, He is always there.

If we want to turn thoughtful doubt into heartfelt belief, we must spend more time in God's Word. His Word answers questions that enable the Spirit to stir our heart. It develops spiritual strength beyond what we thought capable. This is why it's vital we not simply read the Bible, but study God's Word. We need to acquire as much knowledge, understanding, and wisdom, as possible. It's what develops faith. Faith is what we need to stop overthinking, giving way to the heart and what we spiritually feel.

Since the Bible is such an important part of God's provisions, we need to understand how it was written. Some writers were describing events they actually witnessed. Some heard God's voice. Some saw visions, or had dreams. But no matter the circumstances, every writer was inspired by God to step out in faith. They literally put their lives on the frontline to spread the Word of God. Second Timothy

3:16–17 says, "All Scripture is inspired by God and is useful to teach us what is true and to make us realize what is wrong in our lives. It corrects us when we are wrong and teaches us to do what is right. God uses it to prepare and equip his people to do every good work." Thanks to the courage of these writers we have the opportunity to understand what is true, what is wrong in our lives, and how to correct it. As a part of God's perfect plan, the Bible has survived the test of time to document real-life stories, astounding events, and miracles. We are living proof of the continuation and fulfillment of God's plan. Don't you want to be a part of God's perfect plan? Then make the effort to gain the knowledge and wisdom God's Word provides. Don't let the courage of these writers go to waste by ignoring such a precious gift from God. Instead, have the courage to step out in faith, to embrace a God who is real, a God who is alive.

Because we live in a time of instantly shared information, it's hard for us to imagine a time without the internet, TV, radio, and smart phones. When the Bible was written, we weren't able to instantly write things down. Information was passed along by word of mouth. Eventually, much of what was witnessed, was documented and transcribed to become the Bible we read today. When you read the Bible, think of the writers as journalist documenting what was actually happening at the time. First John 1:1–4 says, "We proclaim to you the one who existed from the beginning, whom we have heard and seen. We saw him with our own eyes and touched him with our own hands. He is the Word of life. This one who is life itself was revealed to us, and we have seen him. And now we testify and proclaim to you that he is the one who is eternal life. He was with the Father, and then he was revealed to us. We proclaim to you what we ourselves have actually seen and heard so that you may have fellowship with us. And our fellowship is with the Father and with his Son, Jesus Christ. We are writing these things so that you may fully share our joy." John is speaking in the present tense, for multiple witnesses. *They* are proclaiming the existence of God. *They* saw and touched a living God. *They* knew He was the Word of God in the flesh. *They* knew He was once with the Father. *They* witnessed a risen and living Jesus after His death. Thank God for the faithfulness of these writers to document the Truth. Because of their courage, we have the knowledge and the wisdom we need to embrace this same living and loving God.

We need to wholeheartedly embrace the Truth. We need to rely on the strength of the Spirit, to develop the faith we need to believe this man named Jesus, is in fact the Son of God. We need to have the faith to believe the Son of God performed miracles and miraculous healings, knowing everything would be witnessed, documented, and shared. In biblical days, it was safer to deny God, because the writers faced the possibility of persecution and death. This in itself is a true testament of how important it is for us to know the Truth. If we deny the Spirit, we will lack the faith to believe Jesus was the Son of God. Satan, the Father of Lies, will spiritually attack to influence us to believe all the historical accounts, although witnessed by many different people, are lies.

So if you have even a spark of faith, you must develop that spark by embracing the Truth, God was crucified, God died, God was raised from the dead, and God is alive. You must embrace the Truth that everything we experience is by the grace of God. Faith in God leads to trusting God. Trusting God leads to knowing God. Knowing God leads to a better understanding of who He is. You will be able to make sense out of the knowledge gained. Then, by applying the knowledge to your life, you can begin to experience everything God has planned. Psalm 32:8–9 says, "The Lord says, 'I will guide you along the best pathway for your life. I will advise you and watch over you. Do not be like a senseless horse or mule that needs a bit and bridle to keep it under control.'" Are you acting like a jackass?

Do you struggle with believing in God because you don't know for sure He is alive? How do you know for sure He isn't? If you're on the fence, why would you choose not to believe? Does your pride get in the way because you can't intellectually figure it out? Does your personal desire or agenda get in the way? Are you more interested in earthly pleasures than obeying and following God? Are you more interested in immediate gratification than you are with a long-lasting relationship with God? Are you paying more attention to Satan than you are to the Spirit? These questions need to be addressed for you to figure out what it's going to take for you to believe and have an increase of faith.

Your lack of faith allows the devil to continue to have a foothold on your life. You must stop listening to the evil one. You must get rid of ego and pride, personal desire and agenda, earthly pleasures and immediate gratification. You must acknowledge the existence of the Holy Spirit, the living God in you, and recognize that much of what you feel is from the Spirit of God. By acknowledging these truths, your life will begin to take on new meaning. You'll experience life like you've never experienced or imagined.

Faith not only affects life here on Earth, but you can begin to look forward to spiritual life eternal. That's right, let's not forget the promise of life eternal for those who believe. Romans 6:23 says, "For the wages of sin is death, but the free gift of God is eternal life through Christ Jesus our Lord." John 3:15 says, "So that everyone who believes in him will have eternal life." We need to claim this free gift of eternal life through Jesus, by believing!

Don't misunderstand. We will continue to struggle with our personal thoughts, desires, and feelings. We will continue to fight spiritual battles, as the evil one tries to stifle what we hear from the Holy Spirit. It's how we respond to these struggles and battles that define who we are in Christ. As followers of Christ, we know God is alive, because the Spirit of God lives in us. We can feel His presence as He influences our mind, touches our heart, and affects our actions. When we acknowledge the Spirit of God actively influencing our lives, it motivates us to make more of an effort to know God better. The more we know God, the more our relationship with Him will grow, the deeper we will love Him. Start today. Start right now. Start making the personal effort to know God better.

13

Knowing God

Getting to know someone is a process. It's how relationships develop. It starts with an encounter at work, school, the neighborhood, church, or a social activity. Once we discover common interests with others, it results in the desire to spend more time together. Over time relationships are formed, but they're shallow, and they should be. A shallow relationship doesn't mean it isn't good, it simply means it isn't deep. It provides an opportunity to just hang out and have fun, without all the drama. As you spend more time with someone, you can then decide whether you are interested in a deeper, more meaningful relationship. If so, you must be willing to invest the time and effort needed, to gain insight into their true character.

One of the most common reasons why so many relationships fail is we pursue a deeper relationship without knowing someone's true character. We don't get to know someone's true character by what they say they would do in real life. Because action speaks louder than words, someone's true character is revealed by what they actually do in real life. Once we know someone's true character, we can then decide whether to pursue a more meaningful relationship, or just keep it shallow. Once we go too deep with someone, and later discover their true character is not very appealing, it may be emotionally difficult to get out of the relationship.

Another reason for so many failed relationships is we simply ignore someone's true character. We can become so desperate for a deeper and more meaningful relationship, we ignore the warning signs. We make excuses for their actions. They're not really like that; they're just having a bad day. It was a onetime thing. They will change. Or we think we can change them. We must base our pursuit of a deeper and more meaningful relationship on someone's true character. This is how caring and trusting friendships are formed, that have the potential of developing into loving relationships.

Knowing God is a similar process. Well, except for the obvious, He is God. But we still must be willing to invest the amount of time necessary to gain insight into His true character. Because action speaks louder than words, God's true character is revealed by His action. He sent His Son to die on the cross, to pay for our sin, to give us the opportunity to be back in a relationship with Him. He raised Christ from the grave, showing us the way to spiritual life eternal. He sent the Holy Spirit to live in us. God's true character is not only revealed by what He did for us, it's revealed by what He continues to do for us. This should spiritually inspire and motivate us to pursue a deeper and more meaningful relationship with Him.

In John 15:13–15, Jesus says, "There is no greater love than to lay down one's life for one's friends. You are my friends if you do what I command. I no longer call you slaves, because a master doesn't confide in his slaves. Now you are my friends, since I have told you everything the Father told me." Thanks to the Word of God, we know everything the Father told Jesus. Therefore, if we are willing to do what He commands, we are included in this friendship. Do you know any greater love and friendship than this? If your relationship with God remains shallow and fails to develop into a trusting and loving friendship, you can't say you didn't have the opportunity to know God's true character. Here's some irony for you. God knows your true character, yet He pursues you anyway. He pursues you because He knows you are a work in progress. He'll never give up on you. Isn't this the kind of loving relationship you should be pursuing with all your heart? Why in the world would you want to miss this? Why wouldn't you want to invest whatever time and effort it takes to get to know Him better?

You are one of the countless reasons God provides His Word. He wants you to gain insight, understanding, and be spiritually motivated to personally know Him. You must be willing to humble yourself. After all, He already knows your true character. What do your thoughts, feelings, and actions, reveal about your true character? Does your true character reveal you're more interested in what the world thinks, than what God thinks? Does your true character reveal you're more interested in being in a relationship with the world, than in a relationship with God?

Although God's Word is by far the best way to know Him, how else might we know Him? Romans 1:19–20 says,

"They know the truth about God because he has made it obvious to them. For ever since the world was created, people have seen the earth and sky. Through everything God made, they can clearly see his invisible qualities—his eternal power and divine nature. So they have no excuse for not knowing God." We know God when we see the beauty and splendor of a sunrise or sunset. We know God by the perfection in the color and pattern of a flower, or butterfly wing. We know God by exploring the depth of the oceans, or observing the majestic mountains. We know God by studying all creation, the human body, the plants and animals, the Earth and all the galaxies.

We also know God by acknowledging Him in our ability to advance in the disciplines of science and medicine. This is all a part of His plan for us. Not to just survive, but to prosper and live life abundant. We know God by acknowledging Him in our ability to grow, process, and preserve food. We know God by acknowledging Him in our ability to erect complex water systems and electrical grids. We know God by acknowledging Him in the medical advances of treating and curing disease. We know God by acknowledging Him in every blessing He provides. Is there any excuse for not knowing God?

God blesses us with the ability to acquire knowledge and gain understanding. But can we be too smart for our own good? Can we begin to think we have the ability to fully understand God and creation? Then, when we can't figure it out, Satan influences us to believe it must not be true. We can find ourselves denying God in everything. We will always fall short of fully understanding everything

God. Some questions will remain unanswered. This is exactly why we need to depend more on heartfelt faith than thoughtful understanding. Living by faith is the ability to let our intellectual guard down to embrace how truly amazing God is. Hebrews 11:3 says, "By faith we understand that the entire universe was formed at God's command, that what we now see did not come from anything that can be seen."

Genesis 1:27 says, "So God created human beings in his own image. In the image of God he created them; male and female he created them." By faith, we know God is the creator of the entire universe. By faith, we know God created us. By faith, we know God gave us eyes to see, ears to hear, and a brain to comprehend, so we could see Him, hear Him, and know Him. By faith, we know our loving God was crucified on the cross, so we could know His love for us. By faith, we know we are able to procreate and evolve into a people of relationship, because God created us for relationship. By faith, we know the Holy Spirit lives in us to spiritually transform us. By faith, we know God.

Because God created us with free will, we can choose to deny God in everything. We can choose to believe God can be found in nothing. Nothing was purposefully created or intended, and everything is just by chance. We can choose to believe, the perfect position of the sun, and how it provides perfect warmth and light, is just by chance. We can choose to believe, how the Earth rotates on its axis in perfect harmony with the universe, and its position in the solar system, is just by chance. We can choose to believe, the gravity that keeps us grounded, and the perfect blend of the air we breathe, is just by chance. Isn't it extremely naïve for us to think all of these complex systems, are just by chance?

Instead of choosing to believe everything is just by chance, why not take a chance on God? Is there a chance you are seeing all the color and wonder of creation through the eyes of a created being? Is there a chance everything you are able to experience has been provided by God? Is there a chance our ability to acquire knowledge and develop wisdom is God-given? Is there a chance our emotions and the ability to feel from the heart are because the Holy Spirit lives in us?

Just as in any relationship, the more we know God, the more we will love and trust Him. We know we can trust His love because He first loves us. He is the true love experience. Until you have experienced the true love of God, you will never know what true love is, or what it feels like. Once you experience the true love of God, it's important to maintain that love through the strength of the Spirit.

God makes Himself known by the obvious. One of the most obvious is His Word. Thanks to the obedience of every writer, personally inspired by the Spirit of God, we have the ability to gain more insight into knowing and understanding God. The importance of dedicating the necessary time to read and study the Bible cannot be overstated. God provides His Word to spiritually inspire us to pursue a deeper and more meaningful relationship with Him.

We need to study God's Word to gain as much wisdom as possible. We need the strength of the Holy Spirit for the courage to apply this wisdom to our lives. Proverbs 3:13–18 says, "Joyful is the person who finds wisdom, the one who gains understanding. For wisdom is more profitable than silver, and her wages are better than gold. Wisdom is more precious than rubies; nothing you desire can compare with her. She offers you long life in her right hand, and riches and honor in her left. She will guide you down delightful paths; all her ways are satisfying. Wisdom is a tree of life to those who embrace her; happy are those who hold her tightly." Do you want to be joyful and happy? Do you want something more profitable and precious than silver, gold, or rubies? Do you want long life, riches, and honor? Do you want guidance and satisfaction? Then be wise enough to do everything you can to know God, because God is love.

14

God Is Love

Before we are physically born into this world, while living in the womb, we depend on our mother for survival. After we are born, our physical dependence slowly transitions to an emotional dependence. As we age, we develop the desire to become more independent. If our physical and emotional dependence on our mother was positive and healthy, as we become more independent, our relationship with our mother should remain positive and healthy. It should be one of trust, which means being able to depend on our mother, no matter the circumstances. This trusting relationship with our mother is our first love experience. This is why the bond between a mother and a child is like no other. This love experience should be further enhanced by the love of our father and extend throughout the entire family.

The family, another one of God's provisions, is lovingly responsible to hold family members accountable for their actions. This does not mean family love should be conditional or judgmental. Judgment causes family members to turn their backs on other family members because of faults, failures, mistakes, or choices they don't agree with. Families should love one another through faults, failures, mistakes, and the choices they don't agree with. Judgment is hopeless; love is hopeful.

God's provision of the family is but a glimpse into the depth of His love. Jeremiah 1:5 says, "I knew you before I formed you in your mother's womb. Before you were born I set you apart and appointed you as my prophet to the nations." Our love experience with God goes much deeper than the womb and way beyond the grave. Our love experience with God is spiritual, so it relies on the Holy Spirit. If we rely on the Spirit, our love experience with God will develop into a trusting relationship. Trust faithfully believes we can depend on God, no matter the circumstances. Our relationship with God is our first *true* love experience, because God's love is faithfully unconditional. This means without fail, God loves us through our faults, failures, mistakes, and choices.

Because God is love, His design of the family is an extension of His love. If the love of God is present in the family, the love we receive from our mother, father, and extended family, will shine the Light of God's love. This gives us insight and understanding into God's love. If the love of God is absent in the family, the family will struggle. Based on how many families struggle, how present is God's love in the family today?

As part of God's true love experience, when we accept Jesus Christ as our Savior, He gives us the opportunity to be born again of the Spirit. In John 3:3 Jesus says, "I tell you the truth, unless you are born again, you cannot see the Kingdom of God. In John 3:5–7 Jesus says, "I assure you, no one can enter the Kingdom of God without being born of water and the Spirit. Humans can reproduce only human life, but the Holy Spirit gives birth to spiritual life. So don't be surprised when I say 'You must be born again.'" Being born of the Spirit is the beginning of spiritual life eternal. It means having the strength of the Holy Spirit in us, which helps us fully experience the true love of God.

If the love of the family is founded on the love of God, a common thread of trust runs through the family. This same common thread of trust runs through the family of God. Isn't it awesome, we can be members of both our immediate family, and the family of God? The family of God includes all believers, often referred to as brothers and sisters in Christ. Just as in our human family, the family of God is also lovingly responsible to hold its family members accountable for their actions. This does not mean the love of God's family should be conditional, as this would imply judgment. The family of God should love one another through faults, failures, mistakes, and personal choices. As members of God's family, we should always have someone to depend on through all the seasons of our life, the good, the bad, and the ugly.

Because we are not perfect, and vulnerable to the attacks of Satan, our execution of God's plan for the family often falls short. We fail to obey God, and we judge and turn our backs on family members because of their personal choices. We give in to our sinful nature and fail to love the way God commands us to love. Because our love is conditional, it becomes hopeless. The family must continuously strive to imitate God's love, by never failing to offer Godly love. Godly love is unconditional. It's always hopeful.

Our love should be a beacon of Light into the darkness for the hopeless to find hope. In John 3:16–17 Jesus says, "For this is how God loved the world: He gave his one and only Son, so that everyone who believes in him will not perish but have eternal life. God sent his Son into the world not to judge the world, but to save the world through him." Thanks to God's love, and His design of the family, we can feel the emotion of a Father giving His one and only Son as a sacrifice. Ephesians 2:4–5 says, "But God is so rich in mercy, and he loved us so much, that even though we were dead because of our sins, he gave us life when he raised Christ from the dead. (It is only by God's grace that you have been saved!)" This gives us great insight into knowing God is love. He loves us even though we are all sinners, and all fall short in offering Godly love to ourselves and others. He loves us because we are His children.

Although what we have done, the works we do, and our church attendance all matter to God, it's not a condition of His love. We can't earn our way to being saved. You might think you're not worthy, you don't deserve it, and you'd be right. The only way we are made worthy, is through the loving gift of atonement, provided by the final sacrifice of the Son of God. God loves us so much, that He provides the only way to bring us back into a loving relationship with Him. In John 14:6 Jesus says, "I am the way, the truth, and the life. No one can come to the Father except through me."

How have you responded to the Truth that God loves you unconditionally? Is your love for Him unconditional? How much do you love Him compared to how much He loves you? How do you show your love for God, compared to how He shows His love for you? Is your love for God based on how well you perceive your life is going? Is it based on how well you think He's answering your prayers? When good things are happening in your life, is your love for God stronger than when things aren't going so well? Do you forget God in the good times, and run to Him in the bad? Do you praise God in the good times, and curse Him in the bad?

We tend to approach our relationship with God, the way we approach our earthly relationships. If someone we love upsets us by not responding the way we think they should, we resent and withdraw from them. Have you noticed how quickly pride rears its ugly head, creating disputes between loved ones? How many severed relationships? The devil will use the opportunity to spiritually attack, because he knows a family divided is a family vulnerable. The longer Satan can keep family members separated, the better chance of completely destroying their relationship, and ultimately affecting their relationship with God. We will begin to question where God is in all of this. Do you react to God in the same way you react in your earthly relationships? If you feel He isn't giving you what you want, think you need, or deserve, do you resent God and withdraw from Him? Here's the Good News. No matter how your love waivers for God, His love remains constant.

Life as we know it is not always a bowl of cherries, or a walk in the park. It can be very challenging, because we don't know what's around the corner. In a split second we could encounter calamity, misfortune, hardship, or disaster that can result in pain, suffering, and sadness. We must learn to depend on God and trust Him to love us through the challenging times of our life. By the strength of God, we can persevere and come out on the other side stronger. When times are good, we need to stop and enjoy every moment and thank God for His blessings. When times are not so good, we need to lean on God, to help us through the pain, suffering, and sadness.

Philippians 1:29 says, "For you have been given not only the privilege of trusting in Christ but also the privilege of suffering for him." Suffering a privilege? When we encounter hardships, pain and suffering, do we think of it as a privilege? But as Christ suffered for us, we must suffer for Christ. Our pain and suffering connects us to His pain and suffering. He hung on a cross and died a slow agonizing death as if He had committed unpardonable sins. This should have been our destiny, our cross to bear, not His. Yet He took our place. He took the burden of our sin, because God is love. So as we suffer, we should always be reminded of how God suffered for us, because He loves us. When we suffer, Satan wants us to embrace the darkness, but God wants us to embrace the Light. God is the difference between the darkness and the Light.

Why can't life be a bowl of cherries, or a walk in the park? Why is there so much pain and suffering? It all goes back to the original sin, when we were cast out of the garden into an existence of sin and decay. Because God is love, He provided a way back into a relationship with Him, through His Son, Jesus Christ. He provides the Bible, so we can know the Truth. He provides the Holy Spirit for the guidance we need to find joy. Yes, even in our suffering we can find joy. First Peter 1:6–7 says, "So be truly glad. There is wonderful joy ahead, even though you must endure many trials for a little while. These trials will show that your faith is genuine. It is being tested as fire tests and purifies gold—though your faith is far more precious than mere gold. So when your faith remains strong through many trials, it will bring you much praise and glory and honor on the day when Jesus Christ is revealed to the whole world." By keeping our focus on God's love, our faith enables us to endure anything this life throws at us, because we have praise, glory, and honor, to look forward to.

It's important we understand how to transition the love of God to our earthly relationships. Godly love is the heartfelt emotion of love, guided by the Spirit of God. If love is not heartfelt, and guided by the Spirit, love becomes more about what we humanly think, and less about how we spiritually feel. Godly love is more about what we spiritually feel and less about what we humanly think. First Corinthians 13:4–7 says, "Love is patient and kind. Love is not jealous or boastful or proud or rude. It does not demand its own way. It is not irritable, and it keeps no record of being wronged. It does not rejoice about injustice but rejoices whenever the truth wins out. Love never gives up, never loses faith, is always hopeful, and endures through every circumstance." Everyone gets so emotional when these Bible verses are read during the wedding ceremony to set the love tone of marriage. Reality check, how many marriages end up failing? What causes these failures? When you examine your past relationships of love, did you love the way God says to love? If you examine your current relationships of love, do you love the way God says to love? It's never too late. Just as God's love reunited us in relationship with Him through Jesus Christ, God's love can reunite us in relationship with one another.

When we find ourselves in the trying times of our love relationships, it's an opportunity to show our faith is strong and our faith is genuine. We can show our trust and love for God, by how we love one another. By trusting and loving God, we can find peace and comfort in knowing, there is wonderful joy ahead. But if we respond to the trying times of our love relationships with grumbling and complaining, we are showing a lack of faith, a lack of trust, and a lack of love for God. We are showing a love not founded on God.

Why is it so hard for us to love the way God commands us to love? Is our faith weak? Is our faith false? Is it our pride? If Satan's spiritual attacks continue to be successful, we will see even more severed relationships. Our families, our communities; our cities, our states, and the world will continue to suffer. But if we rely on the Spirit of God to guide us through the ups and downs of our relationships, we will be more successful with the emotions associated with loving and being loved. Once we stabilize our relationships, we will find stability in ourselves and all aspects of our life. We will understand who we truly are in Christ. We will gain insight and understanding into what God's purpose is for our life. Wouldn't you love to know what God's purpose is for your life?

15

God's Gifts and God's Calling

God's gifts are the abilities, skills, and talents we use in all aspects of our lives. God's calling is revealed by our willingness to use our gifts to further the Kingdom of God. Whether we are called to minister, teach, mentor, witness, or serve, when we answer God's calling, it leads to a more meaningful and fulfilling life. His purpose for our life can also be revealed. Are you living a meaningful and fulfilling life? Do you feel good about what you're doing? Do you feel like God is blessing it? Are you blessing others? If you're being honest with yourself and God, you'll know if you're on the right path. If you're not where you want to be in life, then it's possible you're not using God's gifts the way God intended. Or you're not answering God's calling, according to His plan.

To have any hope of understanding how to use God's gifts, to answer God's calling, to fulfill God's plan, we must better understand God's Word, and how to apply His Way to our life. To gain insight and understanding into what God is doing in our life, we must acknowledge the Holy

Spirit and the guidance He provides. We must give the glory to God for our abilities and all we achieve. If our faith is weak, we are more likely to ignore the Spirit's guidance and follow Satan's lead. This leads to a prideful demeanor and sinful behavior. We will fail to understand and apply God's Word to our life. We will not follow God's plan. It will lead to calamity and everyone out for themselves. Doesn't this look and sound familiar today? Aren't we seeing more self-ish, prideful, and sinful behavior?

We need to dig deep to feel the Spirit within us. The Spirit will encourage and motivate us to acknowledge, God is indeed the provider of all things. He gives us the ability to be who He wants us to be. He has given us specific gifts enabling us to achieve everything through Him, as deter-mined by Him. Yes, determined by Him. We are all a part of His plan, and how we respond to His plan determines how well we use our gifts. In Romans 12:7–8 Paul says, "If your gift is serving others, serve them well. If you are a teacher, teach well. If your gift is to encourage others, be encouraging. If it is giving, give generously. If God has given you leadership ability, take the responsibility seri-ously. And if you have a gift for showing kindness to others, do it gladly." We must not only identify our gifts, we must use them well. Since we don't always know what God's plan is, we must remain faithful to follow the Spirit's lead, and trust God is in control.

Not everyone is called to use their gifts specifically in the church. God provides the opportunity to use our God-given gifts to serve, teach, encourage, give, lead, and show kindness, outside the church. There are a multitude of callings that lead to other professions that allows us to use our gifts effectively. Some are called to support others who are answering their calling. No matter how we use our gifts, what a special blessing to use them within our chosen profession, to answer God's calling to further the Kingdom of God.

We might be musically gifted and called to professionally play an instrument, sing, write, or produce music. We might be artistically gifted and called to professionally create art, act, or write. We might be called to become a doctor or scientist, because we are gifted with the ability to learn and comprehend. We might be gifted with a servant's heart and are called into nursing, the military, or food service. We might be gifted with a compassionate heart and are called to counsel those in need of emotional and spiritual guidance.

God gives gifts to be used for what He intends them to be used for. Are you using your gifts the way God intended them to be used? Are you helping or encouraging others? Are you bringing joy to other people? Are you helping to improve the condition of the planet? Are you helping improve the condition of life? Do you honestly believe what you're doing would be pleasing to God? If you don't feel good about what you're doing, or you don't believe it would please God, then you need to reevaluate what you're doing and why you're doing it.

If you're not blessed to use your gifts within your chosen profession, then use your gifts outside the workplace. Volunteering is an excellent way to use your gifts for what God intends. You can sing in the church choir, mentor a student, work in a food bank or shelter. You can be a good neighbor, give to charity, or help someone in need. If you've identified your gifts, every response in life is in some way, a part of God's ultimate plan. It's a big world, with many intricate parts. There's no way for us to know how God is causing all things to come together. We all need to do our part. If we do our part, all things will come together for the good God intends. It's why He gives gifts in the first place.

God is perfect and He created us in His image. Who are we to question or challenge Him? We get so caught up in the ways of this world, we think if we don't look a certain way, or don't succeed in a certain way, we're inferior. Why do we look to everyone else for validation? When we do something special, why do we look around to see if someone is watching? Why do we care so much about what everyone else thinks? The answer is we shouldn't. After all, what makes others the authority? They're just fellow human beings navigating their way through life just like we are.

Although recognition and approval from our fellow human beings can be pleasing and motivating, we must always remember to look to God first. Our validation should come from God. He is the all-powerful and all-knowing creator. He is the King of kings, and Lord of lords. We should be interested in what God thinks. We are uniquely individual by design. We are uniquely gifted through God's blessings. We must take a stand on the frontline, for our right to be who we are in Christ. We must stand for what we believe. When we allow others to influence us, and we don't embrace our individuality, our uniqueness, and our gifts, we can miss God's purpose for our life.

When trying to identify your gifts, don't get caught up in comparing yourself to others. No matter how bad you think you want it, you're not supposed to be like anyone else. Your gifts are unique to you, and their gifts are unique to them. Everything about you is a personal gift from God. Your hair, your teeth, your skin, your eyes, and your body size, all make you unique. As imperfect beings living in an imperfect world, we find ourselves wanting to improve our appearance, and it's usually based on what someone else perceives as better. While there's certainly nothing wrong with wanting to look better, start by simply taking better care of yourself. Don't attempt to change things that are profoundly you. Your hair may not be as full and as shiny as someone else's. Your body size, no matter how hard you try, may never be as small as someone else's. None of this superficial stuff matters. What really matters is what's going on inside. How beautiful is your Spirit? How kind and caring are you? How is your personal relationship with Christ? It's the spiritual stuff that makes you truly happy. It enables you to experience true joy and peace. To live life abundantly, as God intends you to live.

If you're where you want to be in life, and God is an important part of it, this is a good indication you're effectively using God's gifts. It's also a good indication you are answering God's calling, and might be on the right path to fulfilling God's plan. If you're not where you want to be in life, and God is still an important part of it, you need to remain faithful and trust He has a plan. Keep identifying God's gifts and be ready to use them when He calls.

If you're where you want to be in life, and God is not an important part of it, you're probably not using God's gifts effectively. You're most likely not on the right path to fulfilling God's plan. God needs to be an important part of your life. Without Him, you will most likely miss opportunities to use His gifts to answer His calling. If you're doing something that doesn't necessarily make you happy but gives you the means needed to provide for yourself, or your family, find peace in knowing you are providing. Peace brings joy in knowing, that what you're doing brings honor to yourself and God. This is a good indication you're probably right where you need to be, at this particular time in your life. If you don't have peace and joy in what you're doing, and it doesn't bring honor to yourself and God, it's time to reevaluate.

Tomorrow isn't promised, so don't miss the opportunity to follow Christ today. We only get one chance to live this life. We don't want to look back and wish we had done things differently. It's never too late to change direction. God is always with us. We should be confident that no matter where we find ourselves, God still has a plan. We should watch for God to direct our path. He could be opening a door we didn't know existed, or He could be closing one He doesn't want us to walk through. He could be providing a path we didn't see, or He could be providing an out, at just the right time. Proverbs 3:5–6 says, "Trust the Lord with all your heart; do not depend on your own understanding. Seek his will in all you do, and he will show you which path to take."

Everybody discovers their gifts at different times in their lives. God knows what we're doing, and He is spiritually transforming us into who He intends us to be. We all can't work in a job that is best suited to use our gifts to the fullest. So we must look for opportunities to use our God-given gifts within the work setting. Maybe at this time in your life, God is using you to support and assist someone else with their calling. We must continue to follow the Spirit's lead to obey God, because we don't always know His ultimate plan. Remember, it's about His will, not ours. It's about His timing, not ours. Be patient, keep discovering, and stay focused.

God has a plan, and we are all an important part of it. If God is a part of your life, you should be able to find joy, no matter the circumstances. Joy is a byproduct of truly embracing our relationship with Christ. We should be joyfully shining our Light, and inspiring those around us. The key is to depend on God in all circumstances. It's not about what we don't have; it's about what we do have. It's about who we are in Christ. It's about how we live our life. It's about our faith and trust in God. This is what it means to have abundant life.

16
Abundant Life

Jesus says He came so we can have life, and have it more abundantly. What comes to your mind when you think about abundant life? Do you think about money, a house, a car, or nice clothes? Do you think about health? Do you think about looks? Do you think it's only the wealthy, or the best-looking people, who have abundant life? Living life abundant is not about wealth. The wealthiest can live a life of misery. It's not about looks. The most beautiful in appearance can be the ugliest on the inside. When Jesus teaches about abundant life, He's referring to spiritual joy with God. Without God, we are destined to miss what it means to be spiritually joyful. Only through the Spirit of God, can we truly know and experience, what it means to have abundant life. It's dependent upon our personal relationship with Christ.

Despite our belief in God and our relationship with Christ, the great choices we make, what we do right or wrong, there will be seasons in our life. Seasons refer to every aspect of our lives, the ups and downs, the good and bad. In Acts 1:7 Jesus says, "The Father alone has the authority to set those dates and times, and they are not for you to know." Ecclesiastes 3:1–8 says, "For everything there is a season, a time for every activity under heaven. A time to be born and a time to die. A time to plant and a time to harvest. A time to kill and a time to heal. A time to tear down and a time to build up. A time to cry and a time to laugh. A time to grieve and a time to dance. A time to scatter stones and a time to gather stones. A time to embrace and a time to turn away. A time to search and a time to quit searching. A time to keep and a time to throw away. A time to tear and a time to mend. A time to be quiet and a time to speak. A time to love and a time to hate. A time for war and a time for peace."

There are emotions attached to living through the seasons of our lives. At times we will be happy, joyful, and satisfied. At other times, we will be sad, disappointed, and dissatisfied. Life at times will be easy, at other times it will be hard. In John 10:10 Jesus says, "The thief's purpose is to steal and kill and destroy. My purpose is to give them a rich and satisfying life." Jesus wants us to fully understand, Satan does not want us to have abundant life, whereas, He wants us to be happy, joyful, and satisfied. To keep us from abundant life, Satan has been spiritually attacking since the beginning, and he's still attacking today.

Since Jesus came so we may have life and have it abundantly, with God we're hopeful, without God we're hopeless. Ultimately, it's our choice. How are you doing with your choices? Do your choices indicate you are listening to Satan, allowing him to steal, and kill, and destroy? Or do your choices indicate you are listening to the Spirit? Who are you choosing to follow, Satan and the world, or Christ?

Abundant life is achieved through our relationship with Christ and our dependence on the Spirit. It's easy to think we're living life abundant when all is going well. But abundant life can be achieved through God's peace, even while living through the difficult seasons of our life.

Let's get real. As we suffer through sickness, and the prescribed medicine that makes us feel worse than the sickness itself, how do we find peace? As we watch loved ones suffer through sickness, especially a parent watching helplessly as their child suffers, how do we find peace? When a child is unexpectedly taken from us as a result of an illness or accident, how do we find peace? We find peace in the promise of Jesus Christ, that no matter what we encounter in this life, there is the promise of life eternal in the Spirit. This life we're living is but a moment in time compared to eternity. When we or someone we love are suffering, it's hard to think about spiritual life eternal. But God's Word reminds us, through Christ, victory over death is ultimately ours.

If we choose to believe life is just what we see, with no God and no eternal life, we will not have peace. There is nothing to look forward to. We live, we suffer, and we die. If we choose to believe there is a loving God, there's more to life than what meets the eye, and there's spiritual life eternal, we will find peace. There is everything to look forward to. We live, we suffer, we die, and we have eternal life with God. God understands everything we're going through because He experienced life in the flesh. He walked with us and talked with us. He knows what it's like to be human. He suffered and died for us. He felt more physical and emotional pain than most of us will ever feel or imagine. He did this because He loves us, and He wants to save us. He conquered the grave so we could witness spiritual life after physical death. In Revelation 1:18 Jesus says, "I am the living one. I died, but look—I am alive forever and ever! And I hold the keys of death and the grave."

As you live the seasons of your life, as you make choices to follow this world or follow Christ, how do you feel on a day to day basis? What makes you happy? What brings you peace? If you're troubled by how you feel, where is God in your life? Is He an active part of your life? Is God more important than anything else in your life? First John 2:15–17 says, "Do not love this world nor the things it offers you, for when you love the world, you do not have the love of the Father in you. For the world offers only a craving for physical pleasure, a craving for everything we see, and pride in our achievements and possessions. These are not from the Father, but are from this world. And this world is fading away, along with everything that people crave. But anyone who does what pleases God will live forever." To have the love of the Father in you, you must not love the world.

We can maintain our presence in the world and still be recognized as different. We should be noticeably different because of our belief in God, our personal relationship with Christ, and our dependence on the Spirit. While maintaining our presence in the world, we might find ourselves challenged by circumstances we can't control, or don't understand. We might feel like God has abandoned us. We must never lose hope. God is always with us. He is always for us. Regardless of our circumstances, God must remain our rock and our foundation. Our response during the most challenging seasons of our life is an important part of our testimony to the world.

As followers of Christ, we all don't have to look alike, or act the same. By God's design, we all look different from one another. Our personalities are unique, and we all don't act alike. We should embrace our individuality and differences. God will use our uniqueness to fulfill His ultimate plan. How boring it would be if everyone looked alike and acted the same. For that reason alone, we should celebrate our differences. We all have something unique to offer, so it's our differences that make us stronger. We are all uniquely a part of God's plan.

When we are young and impressionable, because we want to make friends and belong, we tend to follow the ways of the world. We wear similar clothes and listen to popular music. We use words, phrases, and sentences that take on new meaning. Slang if you will. We follow the trends of the world, like having short or long hair, no matter the gender. There's the trends of men having no facial hair, to just a mustache, to goatees, to full beards, and now to really long beards. No matter the gender, it appears just about everyone is adorning a tattoo or two, or three, or four. We have all been a part of following trends, and it can be fun. But here's the problem. When we choose to follow the world, and it defies common sense, it's a good indication we belong more to this world than we do to God. An example of this is when an individual purposely wears pants so baggy, or so low, their underwear shows. By simple definition, underwear should be worn under our clothes.

By allowing our conformity to the world to define who we are, we lose sight of who we are meant to be in Christ. When our behavior reflects we belong more to the world than we do to God, then it's time to turn back to God. We should never compromise our relationship with Christ, to be in a relationship with the world. Please don't misunderstand, we all need to be a part of society and our culture, but we must maintain our integrity in Christ. He ultimately determines who we truly are and how we should act. We must have more of a desire to please God, than to please the world.

Are you surprised at how difficult and challenging life can be? Reality check, nowhere in the Bible does it tell us, when we follow Christ, we will no longer have difficulty or trouble. Romans 8:35–37 says, "Can anything ever separate us from Christ's love? Does it mean he no longer loves us if we have trouble or calamity, or are persecuted, or hungry, or destitute, or in danger, or threatened with death? (As the Scriptures say, 'For your sake we are killed every day; we are being slaughtered like sheep.') No, despite all these things, overwhelming victory is ours through Christ, who loved us."

The Bible also says, when we choose to follow Christ, we can expect the world to hate us. In John 15:18–19 Jesus says, "If the world hates you, remember that it hated me first. The world would love you as one of its own if you belonged to it, but you are no longer part of the world. I chose you to come out of the world, so it hates you." In Matthew 10:22 Jesus says, "And all nations will hate you because you are my followers. But everyone who endures to the end will be saved." The use of the word *endures* refers to the expectation of challenge. Is there anyone who doesn't feel like life is a challenge?

Within this concept of embracing our individuality and uniqueness in Christ, while enduring what the world throws at us, and as we go through the seasons of our life, we will always need to depend on others. Who do you depend on? Can you depend on your family, your friends, your church family, or your neighbors? Although it's nice to have people you can depend on, when it comes down to faithful dependence in all circumstances, it comes down to God. He is truly a best friend. How about you? Can you depend on yourself in all circumstances? Are you truly your own best friend?

17

I Am, My Best friend

The chapter title has two meanings. You are your best friend, and Jesus Christ, the great I Am, is your best friend. It's easy to understand why you should be your best friend, but how can God, a deity, be your best friend? How does that even make sense? It makes sense because God is a loving God of relationship. In the beginning we enjoyed a personal relationship with Him. Then, because of Satan's influence and our decision to disobey God, we ate the forbidden fruit, and were banished from the garden. We no longer enjoyed a personal relationship with God. Genesis 3:23 says, "So the Lord God banished them from the Garden of Eden, and he sent Adam out to cultivate the ground from which he had been made."

We remained without a personal relationship with God, until He took action and sent His one and only Son to save us. This act alone, gives us the opportunity to be back in a personal relationship with Him. He did this because He knew we could not do it on our own, and He loves us. To help us maintain a personal and loving relationship with Him, He sent the Holy Spirit to live in us. Together, Jesus Christ and the Holy Spirit make

God available and approachable. We can have a bond, an alliance, and a friendship with God. Yes, we can literally have a best friend in Jesus. Why in the world would anyone want to miss this? Why would anyone want to ignore the Spirit and live without God? It comes down to free will. We are all free to embrace God and enjoy a personal relationship with Him, or we can reject and deny Him. To reject and deny God is to reject and deny the Father, the Son, and the Holy Spirit. To reject and deny God is to reject His love, depriving ourselves of a friendship like no other.

As you look at all your relationships, who is your best friend? Without hesitation, who can you depend on? Who knows you best, your deepest thoughts, fears and concerns? Many followers of Christ will quickly answer with the name of Jesus. But in most cases, it's more of a cliché. It's an intellectual response, not heartfelt and truthful. The truth is, not many people can honestly answer with the name of Jesus. Regardless of how we answer, in John 15:13–15, Jesus declares we are His friends by saying, "There is no greater love than to lay down one's life for one's friends. You are my friends if you do what I command. I no longer call you slaves, because a master doesn't confide in his slaves. Now you are my friends, since I have told you everything the Father told me."

Thanks to God for making His Word available, we know everything the Father told Jesus, which is everything Jesus told the disciples. We are included in this friendship if we do what He commands. When Jesus told the disciples there is no greater love than to lay down one's life for one's friends, He was telling them, He will die on the cross for them. He is telling us the same. Do you believe this Truth, God was willing to die for you? Do you believe God considers you His friend? Don't you want to be a part of this friendship? Then you must be willing to make the effort to embrace His friendship. He's done His part, are you doing yours?

If you want to know what it's like to be in a personal relationship with God, if you want a friend in Jesus, it takes a leap of faith. By jumping, what do you have to lose? More importantly, what do you have to find? You would find a relationship that profoundly impacts your life, like no other. You would find a relationship that leads you on a path to spiritual awareness and strength. You would find yourself making better decisions, because you would have the strength of the Holy Spirit to help you battle Satan. You would find you have a better understanding of what God is doing in your life. You would find you have someone to talk to and lean on, to help you get through each and every day. You would find the more godly knowledge you acquire, the more wise you become. Can you believe that you can have a best friend in Jesus, the Son of God?

Now back to the question, who is your best friend? Did you name yourself? Can you depend on yourself? Who do you wake up with every day? Who do you spend every waking moment with? Who is the last person you spend time with before going to sleep? Besides God, who knows you deep within the recesses of your mind and heart? Who knows how you really feel about everything? When you look back on your life, how have you treated yourself? How have you done with the choices you've made and the paths you've taken? Have you taken good care of yourself? Have you acted in your own best interest? Even if you have a best friend in God, you must also be your own best friend.

To be your own best friend, you must always be able to depend on yourself and have your best interest at heart. Stop blaming everyone else for your shortcomings. Stop waiting on everyone else to motivate you. Motivate yourself. Take more of an interest in improving yourself. Read and study the Bible more. Spend more time with God to become more spiritually stimulated and aware. Make better choices. Eat better. Become more physically active. Exercise to become a stronger vessel for God to use. A stronger vessel means being better equipped physically, emotionally, and spiritually. You will be more successful at fighting and winning spiritual battles. Then, as you depend on the strength of the Holy Spirit, you become more confident. God will help you become the person He created you to be.

Have you noticed, when it comes to offering advice to those we care about, the advice is consistently insightful and helpful? Oh, we know what to tell other people. But when it comes to following our own advice, we ignore it. We'll tell someone else to not put off going to the doctor, but we'll put off going. We'll encourage others to exercise and eat right, but we won't exercise and eat right. Why do we have so much trouble self-motivating? We're listening to the whispers and the lies of the devil who's telling us we can't do it, and we're not worthy. We allow Satan to keep us from the plans God has for us. We need to listen to the Spirit of God who is telling us we can do it, and we are worthy. To achieve what we desire for ourselves, we need to use the strength of the Spirit to help us identify and achieve our goals.

What stops you from stepping in a new direction? Are you focusing too much on the big picture? Does the big picture appear to be overwhelming and unachievable? Stop focusing on the big picture and long-term goals, and start focusing on short-term goals. They're not as overwhelming. If you're unhealthy because of what you eat, start making the effort to eat healthier. Don't drastically change everything in a day. Start by cutting down on portion size. Eat less, more frequently. Eat because you need to, not because you want to. Stop eating dinner so late at night. If you have a habit of late night snacking, instead of eating unhealthy sugary snacks, eat healthier snacks like fruit and nuts. At first, cut down on late night snacking, then slowly try to eliminate it.

If you drink six sugary drinks a day, start by cutting it to five, then four, and so on. If you're not used to walking, don't walk a mile, start with walking short distances. If you're a smoker, don't light up another one because it's a habit, put it off until you're struggling and can't put it off any longer. Then, smoke only half. If you drink alcohol, think about why and how much you drink. Cut down on the frequency and the amount you consume. Do you drink to reduce stress? Exercise also reduces stress. Start with light exercise. Don't overdo it. Just make the effort to do better.

Whatever it is you need to do, start today. Stop putting it off. No matter how small the steps appear, it's the small steps that slowly but surely gets you there. You are responsible for your vessel, so start taking responsibility. Stop looking to everyone else to make you happy, make yourself happy. If you have health concerns, your first step should be to contact your doctor's office. Let them know you want to start making changes. They will be excited for you. They will gladly give you advice on how you should safely pursue a healthier and better you.

As you focus on the changes that will make you better, remember, you are in the midst of spiritual battle. Satan is always trying to convince you, you're not worthy. As you try to keep yourself on track, Satan will try to influence you into thinking, you can't do it, you're not able. He'll tell you that you'll fail. He'll influence you to stop trying. After you achieve your goals for a while, if you slip a little, Satan will try to influence you to give up. He'll walk you right back into the darkness where you started.

Instead, if you slip one day, use the strength of the Spirit to get back up again. God will help you regain your confidence through the strength of the Holy Spirit. You have the power of God on your side. When Satan is hitting you with an onslaught of the fiery arrows, pounding you with negativity, you have the knowledge that God is more powerful than Satan. Through God's strength, you can achieve anything. Philippians 4:13 says, "For I can do everything through Christ, who gives me strength."

If Jesus is our best friend, why does the Bible teach us about fearing the Lord? Can we have a best friend in Jesus, yet fear Him at the same time?

18
Fear of the Lord

God is a loving God, and He wants a personal relationship with each and every one of us. He literally wants to be our best friend. Then why would it be necessary to fear Him? Fear is a reverent respect for God's authority. It's the fear of the consequences, when we don't follow the Spirit's lead and fail to obey an all-knowing and all-powerful God. Isn't it interesting, even knowing there will be consequences; we will still choose to follow our sinful desires and Satan's lead? Proverbs 19:23 says, "Fear of the LORD leads to life, bringing security and protection from harm." Luke 1:50 says, "He shows mercy from generation to generation to all who fear him." We find security and protection by fearing the Lord. He shows mercy when we fear Him. So how much do you fear the Lord? Despite knowing what God wants, regardless of the consequences, do you continue to do what you want? How disrespectful.

As children, we all start out life dependent upon others to literally teach us right from wrong. If we're not held accountable for our behavior, we will have problems. Then, as we get older, we will continue to have problems. If we're held accountable for our behavior, we will learn there are consequences associated with our action. Even as we age and mature, we will always be dependent on others for guidance and correction, knowledge and wisdom. Proverbs 1:7–8 says, "Fear of the LORD is the foundation of true knowledge, but fools despise wisdom and discipline. My child, listen when your father corrects you. Don't neglect your mother's instruction."

God's Word teaches us the importance of fear and its connection to wisdom. A child isn't born wise. Matter of fact, as you observe the behavior of children, it can be shocking how naturally selfish and unkind they can be. The importance of a parent taking their responsibility seriously, to instruct and correct their children, cannot be overstated. A father and mother, who embrace their responsibility to instruct and correct their children, will be respectfully feared. As a child, did you fear your father or mother? What were the consequences when you disobeyed? Would there be physical punishment? There's a lot of controversy surrounding a parent's authority and responsibility to discipline their children. God's Word tells us in Proverbs 13:24, "Those who spare the rod of discipline hate their children. Those who love their children care enough to discipline them."

Loving and caring discipline is never about the punishment. It's always about the correction. When disciplining children, it's important to take the necessary time to talk through the consequences associated with their behavior. Discipline does not always have to be physical. There are psychological approaches that also correct behavior. Take away the stuff they love and think they just can't go without.

Insist they take time to be alone to reflect on what they've done. Do whatever needs to be done to get their attention. The fear of consequences is the motivation they need to make better choices. In looking back, was there a lack of discipline or correction in your life? If so, what effect did it have? Do you wish those in positions of authority, would have been more responsible to do things differently?

As we become older, we desire to be more independent. We become less dependent on others. As we take more control of our lives, it doesn't take long before we begin to think we know a lot more than we actually do. This is a critical juncture in our lives, where many of us go astray. Satan uses our pride and sinful nature to spiritually attack us. We focus more on immediate gratification and selfish motives, and ignore much of what we've been taught. We've all suffered the consequences of thinking; we can get away with this, we won't get caught. Next thing we know, we're in trouble.

It's important for us to acknowledge and admit that we never get too old to receive instruction, guidance, correction, and discipline. We can never have too much wisdom. A fool despises wisdom and discipline. As we become more mature and look back on our lives, was anyone as mature as they thought they were at the time? How many of us were foolish enough to despise wisdom and discipline?

No matter our age, we will always be children of God. Galatians 3:26 says, "For you are all children of God through faith in Christ Jesus." John 1:12–13 says, "But to all who believed him and accepted him, he gave the right to become children of God. They are reborn—not with a physical birth resulting from human passion or plan, but a birth that comes from God." No matter our age, we will never outgrow our need to depend on our heavenly Father. We will always need His guidance, wisdom, and correction. He will never leave us. He will always be there for us. Deuteronomy 31:8 says, "Do not be afraid or discouraged, for the LORD will personally go ahead of you. He will be with you; he will neither fail you nor abandon you." Psalm 37:28 says, "For the LORD loves justice, and he will never abandon the godly. He will keep them safe forever, but the children of the wicked will die." How many of us know what it feels like to be physically or emotionally abandoned? Isn't it great to know our heavenly Father promises to never abandon us?

Even knowing there will be consequences, we struggle to obey God. We struggle because we live in a fallen world where evil exists and temptations are plenty. We make bad decisions by following our sinful nature and allowing Satan to influence us. It becomes more about immediate pleasure and self-gratification, and less about God. We find ourselves focusing on earthly pleasures, instead of our spiritual well-being. Satan uses our sinful and prideful demeanor to influence us into thinking we have it all figured out. Proverbs 3:7 says, "Don't be impressed with your own wisdom. Instead, fear the LORD and turn away from evil."

Think about the last time you were considering participating in an activity that would bring shame to yourself or your family. The Spirit of God was telling you one thing, and Satan was telling you another. Did it give you pause? Despite the negative thoughts and feelings, and the possible consequences, did you do it anyway? Or did you decide to stop an ungodly action because of the consequences? When the fear of consequences leads you to obey God, it shows you care about Him. It shows you care about yourself, and you care about those who care about you. It's about self-respect. It's about respect for God. When you disobey God, despite fear of the consequences, it shows you don't care about God. It shows you don't care about yourself, or those who care about you. It shows you lack respect for yourself and God.

Some people have the attitude that nobody should be telling us what to do, or dictate how we live. Some confuse freedom with the right to act the way they want. With respect to governing authorities, the structure of society in which we live, is founded on God. In Mark 12:17 Jesus said, "Well then, give to Caesar what belongs to Caesar, and give to God what belongs to God." Rules and regulations are set forth to keep us safe and help us prosper. Without rules or regulations, social and civil order would be at risk. To maintain order, people in positions of authority are responsible to hold us accountable for our actions. Romans 13:1–2 says, "Everyone must submit to governing authorities. For all authority comes from God, and those in positions of authority have been placed there by God. So anyone who rebels against authority is rebelling against what God has instituted, and they will be punished." How often do we stop and think about what God is trying to accomplish through those in positions of authority? How often do those in positions of authority think about what God is trying to accomplish through them?

God wants us to fear authority. Fear is a sign of respect, knowing we will be held accountable for our actions. When we fear the Lord, parents, teachers, and police, it's a sign of respect for their authority. Romans 13:3–5 says, "For the authorities do not strike fear in people who are doing right, but in those who are doing wrong. Would you like to live without fear of the authorities? Do what is right, and they will honor you. The authorities are God's servants, sent for your good. But if you are doing wrong, of course you should be afraid, for they have the power to punish you. They are God's servants, sent for the very purpose of punishing those who do what is wrong. So you must submit to them, not only to avoid punishment, but also to keep a clear conscience." Is what we see going on in the world today an indication we respect those in authority as God's servants?

Let's get real. There are some people in positions of authority who do not act like God's servants. They abuse their authority and do not deserve respect. But even if we don't respect the person in the position of authority, we must maintain respect for the position. Why? Because people in positions of authority, have the power to negatively affect the lives of the people they govern. We need to remain humble, yet at the same time, hold those in positions of authority accountable for their actions. We need to work the processes in place, to address problems with those who abuse their authority. But no matter what, we must maintain respect for the position.

In looking at society and governing authorities, one of the most concerning problems we face today is the lack of respect between police officers and citizens. Respect is a two-way street. We need to maintain respect for one another. We should not be fearful, just because someone has authority over us. When police approach citizens, we must understand the need for them to be cautious and prepared for the unexpected. But at the same time, they have a responsibility to maintain respect for the innocent. Under normal circumstances, neither the police nor the citizen should have any reason to be fearful. But does anything feel normal these days? When something does go wrong, the consequences can be very dangerous.

Citizens must always be mindful; the police do have a very difficult job. The police must always be mindful, it is a job. They knew the dangers when they accepted the position. They are paid to keep citizens safe and uphold the law. They should do their job without a condescending demeanor or tone. They should be willing to explain their actions as an incident unfolds. But no matter how an officer treats us, we must maintain respect for the position. They are the ones in the position of authority and control. We must always be mindful of how God wants us to act in every situation. Is what we see going on in the world today an indication we have God on our mind?

There's another concerning problem facing society today. When people exercise their right to peacefully assemble, to draw attention to a problem, it's not remaining peaceful. Protests are turning violent, which distracts from the reason they came together in the first place. Instead of the focus being on the cause, it becomes about the violence. We do have the right to peacefully assemble, but we don't have the right to break the law. When violence is evident, we should be evaluating the motives of the organizers, and the individuals involved. We should never compromise our personal integrity, the integrity of the organizers, or the mission of the organization. God's Word is clear. To rebel against authority, is to rebel against what God has instituted. Embedded in our fear of the Lord, is the understanding that all government and authority has evolved under the providence of the Lord. We need to obey God's Word by maintaining respect for government and authority.

What would society be like without governing authorities? What kind of decisions would we make without the fear of consequences? How much worse off would we be considering how bad we are with governing authorities? How much worse can we treat one another? Would we take even more advantage of others? Would we take what we want from those who are weak? If we think back to the earlier times of human existence, we can recall a more barbaric society where they did exactly that. Those who were stronger took people's belongings, land, territory, and kingdoms. Only the strong survived. Thank God for His providence, our growth, and our strength in Him. As a God-fearing nation, we act less like barbarians and more like God-fearing people. Do the decisions and choices you make as an individual reveal you are God-fearing? Do our choices and decisions as a society, a nation, or the world, reveal we are God-fearing? Does what we see covered in the news today reveal we are God-fearing?

Our fear of the Lord is essential in our motivation to obey God. It should keep us from turning sinful thoughts into sinful action. It should keep us from making unwise, unhealthy, and prideful decisions. In Ecclesiastes 12:13–14 Solomon says, "That's the whole story. Here now is my final conclusion: Fear God and obey his commands, for this is everyone's duty. God will judge us for everything we do, including every secret thing, whether good or bad." This should help us to understand, we have a duty to fear God and obey His commands. If we don't fear the Lord, it shows we lack the wisdom to respect Him and His authority. With no fear, no wisdom, and no respect for God, we are on a path to even more sinful and prideful behavior. Sinful and prideful behavior not only affects us individually, but it affects society as a whole. Our fear of the Lord is an important and essential part of our walk with Christ. It helps us become a better person and a better people.

A wise person fears God by understanding we are responsible and will be held accountable for our actions. There will be consequences when we choose to disobey God and His authority. Our actions associated with every decision we make, has a profound influence on every aspect of our lives, and the lives of those around us. It impacts our reality, our spirituality, and our destiny. If we truly believe in God, we need to respectfully fear Him by acknowledging His power and authority. By acknowledging His power and authority, we become more dependent on His strength, and less dependent on our own strength. The more we depend on God, the more we trust Him. Trust leads to peace beyond understanding.

Our God-given response to fear is courage. It takes courage to consistently make godly decisions. It takes courage to make respectful decisions on behalf of ourselves, our families, our friends, and most importantly, the Lord. Fear can show itself in a split second, or it can be a prolonged event. Fear is recognizing the possible consequences associated with every decision we make. Every time we make a wise decision in the face of fear, we are showing we are courageous. Although courage appears to be more evident in the physical realm, it also affects the spiritual realm. Courage won't stop Satan from attacking, but it puts him on notice. It lets him know we depend on God for our strength. God provides every tool necessary to find courage in the face of fear. But to use the tools effectively, we must become stronger in Spirit. To become stronger in Spirit, we must spend more time with God and His Word.

A great place to find opportunities to grow in Spirit is the church. The church is another one of God's provisions. It brings people together, to further His Kingdom. But it's important to understand, what the church is, and what the church isn't.

19
The Church

When we think of the church, a physical building usually comes to mind. But the building itself is not the church. Individuals coming together is the church. Ephesians 2:20 says, "Together, we are his house, built on the foundation of the apostles and the prophets. And the cornerstone is Christ Jesus himself." With Christ as the cornerstone, and the strength of the Holy Spirit, it is our responsibility to continue to build on the foundation of the apostles and the prophets. First Corinthians 6:19–20 says, "Don't you realize that your body is the temple of the Holy Spirit, who lives in you and was given to you by God? You do not belong to yourself, for God bought you with a high price. So you must honor God with your body." First Corinthians 12:27 says, "All of you together are Christ's body, and each of you is a part of it." Individually, we are the temple of the Holy Spirit. Together, we are the body of Christ. United, we are the church.

God does bless us by providing a building to gather. This is the reason church is referred to as God's house, or the house of the Lord. It doesn't matter how small or large, how old or new the building is. Church can be held in a barn or even outside. What matters is we come together to become a beacon of Light into the darkness. So how did we end up with so many different kinds of churches, with so many varying beliefs? It all began with the foundation set by the apostles and prophets, who were on a mission to spread the Good News of Jesus Christ. As the body of Christ grew, individuals began to have different interpretations of the Word of God. Based on the agreement of interpretation and beliefs, followers of Christ began to divide and branch out. Fast forward to today. Can you believe how blessed we are to have so many churches to choose from? Some prefer a church offering a more traditional style of worship and music. Others prefer a more contemporary, or modern style. It doesn't matter the style, what matters is the church's teachings are biblically sound. If so, go and learn from those who are called to teach. Go and enjoy the music, worship the Lord, and be spiritually uplifted. Go and be a part of collectively praying for our communities and our country.

It's important we understand what the church is, and what the church isn't. Church is a place to learn more about God, to gain more insight and understanding into the Word of God, and to receive specific guidance on how to apply God's Word to everyday life. It's a place to gather in small groups to interact with others experiencing similar circumstances and challenges. For example, there are teen groups, single's groups, couple's groups, and family groups. It's an opportunity to share thoughts, concerns, and ideas with other people who are dealing with some of the same things you're dealing with. It's not always easy to navigate our way through this life, and the church is a great place to find the support we need. Small groups allow for a more intimate setting. As more time is spent in small groups, relationships develop and friendships form. We can encourage and support one another.

The church is a great place to develop relationships founded on godly principles. Godly relationships are an important part of improving our lives. As relationships grow, we get to know one another better, and we feel more comfortable. We let our guard down and start allowing others to have more insight into what's really going on in our lives, and who we truly are. We can support one another through life's challenges. Within the context of support, we also have a biblical responsibility to hold each other accountable for our actions. This accountability factor is how deeper friendships develop. It's how we become even more involved as a church family. It can sound weird to think about letting individuals into your personal space, but the church family should be like your regular family. We should be able to depend on each other to get through the hard times, and celebrate the good times.

When you attend church, do you feel spiritually stimulated and encouraged? Do you leave feeling more spiritually inspired than when you came in? Do you leave feeling motivated to learn more about God and to pursue a personal relationship with Christ? Is there an opportunity for you to be a part of community outreach? If the answers are yes, then go deeper by offering more of yourself. If the answers are no, then examine your heart to determine whether you are spiritually ready to receive what the church is offering. If you still feel you haven't found the right church, then keep looking. Every church is not for everybody. It's important to attend church where you are most comfortable, and can truly be yourself. God wants us to come as we are, because He wants to begin a change in us, exactly where we are in life.

If you don't go to church because you don't feel welcomed, then find a church where you do. It's important to attend church where you can be honest with yourself, honest with God, and honest with the church. Honesty allows God to begin a spiritual transformation like you've never experienced. If you attend church, and don't feel like you're a part of God's family, or you don't enjoy the music, or you don't feel spiritually uplifted and inspired, visit other churches. As you visit churches, listen to the Spirit for guidance. Be persistent. There's a church for everyone.

Most people think the church is just about what happens on Sunday. Sunday is important, but it's also about what happens every day in our communities. The church should provide community outreach to help those in need. Outreach is providing companionship for someone alone. It's showing an interest in a teenager's life, so they know someone cares. It's offering emotional support to someone hurting. It's offering financial support to someone going through a tough time. It's going to the frontline in spiritual battle, to help someone gain insight and understanding, into what's going on in their own lives and the world today. It's helping someone understand what it means to have a personal relationship with Christ, and how they can rely on the strength of the Spirit to successfully fight their own spiritual battles. It's about the church shining the Light of Christ into the darkness.

Let's take a look at what the church isn't. The church isn't the fulfillment of every spiritual need. It isn't a replacement for our need to pursue a personal relationship with Christ. It can't fight our personal spiritual battles with Satan. The church isn't a place where its teachings should ever contradict the teachings of the Bible. The church isn't a place to pretend by demeanor, infused with pride, that all is well. This holier-than-thou demeanor is a common complaint against the church, and it causes discord between fellow believers. It also causes potential followers of Christ to feel unworthy, not good enough, and unwelcomed. Ironically, we're all unworthy and not good enough. We all need to remain humble and honestly profess, we're not perfect and we don't have all the answers. Our Light shines brightest when we humbly confess that Jesus Christ is our Lord and Savior, and without Him, we are nothing.

We are all sinners, we all need God, and we all need the church. We all fall short of being worthy without God's grace and forgiveness. First John 1:8–10 says, "If we claim we have no sin, we are only fooling ourselves and not living in the truth. But if we confess our sins to him, he is faithful and just to forgive us our sins and to cleanse us from all wickedness. If we claim we have not sinned, we are calling God a liar and showing that his word has no place in our hearts." Each of us has a past we're not proud of. We're all spiritually transforming, so we're all in a different place when it comes to our personal walk with Christ. Although many put on a brave face in public, we are all hurting. We all go through the ups and downs of life. We all struggle with sin, darkness, and spiritual warfare. We are all trying to make sense out of life. We are all trying to understand why there is so much pain, suffering, and ugliness, and how it can involve a loving God. Here's the Truth. He loves us through the ups and downs, through the struggle, through the pain, through the darkness, and through the ugliness of our sin.

Do you attend church regularly? Are you involved with a church? Does your church offer the opportunity to serve the community? Does your church bring peace to your Spirit? God wants His church to be about furthering His Kingdom. He wants His church to be a welcoming beacon of Light for sinners and lost souls. The church should be a welcoming place. It should be a place to learn about God and His Word. It should stimulate your Spirit and personally motivate you. God took on flesh so He could walk among us to teach humility, service, forgiveness, non-judgment, and love. This was God's way of showing us how we should be with one another, and what the love of the church should look like.

The church affirms Jesus Christ as the cornerstone of faith. Christ came to Earth through the Immaculate Conception, born of a virgin. He took on flesh to fulfill God's ultimate plan, to die as the final sacrifice. He then rose from the dead to live again, which is the key that unlocks the mystery behind all things spiritual. The risen Christ is our only hope of understanding that just as He is spiritual, we too are spiritual. Romans 8:11 says, "The Spirit of God, who raised Jesus from the dead, lives in you. And just as

God raised Christ Jesus from the dead, he will give life to your mortal bodies by this same Spirit living within you." Our belief in Jesus Christ provides the spiritual confidence to know, there is spiritual life after death in the flesh.

Although the church is an important part of our spirituality, God wants us to actively pursue Him on a personal level. He wants us to come to Him exactly as we are. He wants us to feel the Spirit and experience His presence. He wants us to hear Him. He wants us to keep striving to be better today than we were yesterday. The church can't actively pursue Christ for us. It can't feel the Spirit for us. It can't hear God for us. It can't intercede, or speak to God on our behalf. We must depend on our personal effort to truly know God. It's a very personal and loving relationship.

We are all personally responsible to further the Kingdom of God. Do you think God can use you to further the Kingdom? Do you wonder if you're worthy? Although there are countless examples in the Bible where people are used in the most profound ways to further the Kingdom, one of the most profound is the Apostle Paul. If God will use someone like Paul, God will use you.

20

Saul of Tarsus Becomes the Apostle Paul

Throughout the Bible, there are countless examples of how God has this amazing way of using the most unlikely characters to further His Kingdom. The Bible teaches how fishermen like Simon, also called Peter, Andrew, James, and John, became fishers of men. How a young man named Joseph, who was hated and sold into slavery by his brothers, rose to wealth and high position. How a young man named David, was able to kill a giant of a man named Goliath, to illustrate faith and courage beyond human understanding. How Jesus accepted an invitation to the home of a tax collector named Matthew, as an example of how God will spend time with anyone with a desire to spend time with Him. These are just some of the countless examples of how God will use absolutely anyone to further His Kingdom. But one of the most profound examples in the Bible is the Apostle Paul. Paul not only didn't believe that Christ was the Messiah, but he was personally responsible for the persecution of many who did. Yet Christ still used him to influence the world by starting churches and writing many books of the Bible.

Before Paul became a follower of Christ, his name was Saul. He was enthusiastically devoted to persecuting those who were followers of Christ. Acts 8:3 says, "But Saul was going everywhere to destroy the church. He went from house to house, dragging out both men and women to throw them into prison." Acts 9:1–2 says, "Meanwhile, Saul was uttering threats with every breath and was eager to kill the Lord's followers. So he went to the high priest. He requested letters addressed to the synagogues in Damascus, asking for their cooperation in the arrest of any followers of the Way he found there. He wanted to bring them—both men and women—back to Jerusalem in chains." As you can see, Saul was on a personal mission to do everything he could to stop the Lord's followers from furthering the message of Christ.

One day while on the road to Damascus, Jesus had a personal interaction with Saul that would change his life forever. Acts 9:3–9 says, "As he was approaching Damascus on this mission, a light from heaven suddenly shone down around him. He fell to the ground and heard a voice saying to him, 'Saul! Saul! Why are you persecuting me?' 'Who are you, lord?' Saul asked. And the voice replied, 'I am Jesus, the one you are persecuting! Now get up and go into the city, and you will be told what you must do.' The men with Saul stood speechless, for they heard the sound of someone's voice but saw no one! Saul picked himself up off the ground, but when he opened his eyes he was blind. So his companions led him by the hand to Damascus. He remained there blind for three days and did not eat or drink." It's important to note that Saul was Jewish. He believed in the God of the Old Testament. He did not believe that Jesus Christ was God in the flesh, the Savior, the Messiah. So when the voice identified Himself as Jesus, it profoundly influenced his heart.

Do you wonder if God is really in control and on the throne? Let's look at how He provides the right people, at the right time, to fulfill His ultimate plan. Acts 9:10–16 says, "Now there was a believer in Damascus named Ananias. The Lord spoke to him in a vision, calling, 'Ananias!' 'Yes Lord!' he replied. The Lord said, 'Go over to Straight Street, to the house of Judas. When you get there, ask for a man from Tarsus named Saul. He is praying to me right now. I have shown him a vision of a man named Ananias coming in and laying hands on him so he can see again.' 'But Lord,' exclaimed Ananias, 'I've heard many people talk about the terrible things this man has done to the believers in Jerusalem! And he is authorized by the leading priests to arrest everyone who calls upon your name.' But the Lord said, 'Go, for Saul is my chosen instrument to take my message to the Gentiles and to kings, as well as to the people of Israel. And I will show him how much he must suffer for my name's sake.'"

You might be thinking, well if God would speak to me like He did Saul and Ananias, my heart would also be profoundly influenced. But remember, they lived during a time when the Movement was just beginning, and Christ had recently risen from the grave. They were living the New Testament, with little evidence of the Holy Spirit, few churches, and not much of a communications network. We live in a time after Christ ascended back to heaven, and sent the Holy Spirit. We have the New Testament, the Holy Spirit, and churches in every direction. We have a communication network beyond imagination. Believe it or not, we have more opportunities to know God today than ever before.

Let's get back to Saul's story. Acts 9:17–28 says, "So Ananias went and found Saul. He laid hands on him and said, 'Brother Saul, the Lord Jesus, who appeared to you on the road, has sent me so that you might regain your sight and be filled with the Holy Spirit.' Instantly something like scales fell from Saul's eyes, and he regained his sight. Then he got up and was baptized. Afterward he ate some food and regained his strength. Saul stayed with the believers in Damascus for a few days. And immediately he began preaching about Jesus in the synagogues, saying, 'He is indeed the Son of God!' All who heard him were amazed. 'Isn't this the same man who caused such devastation among Jesus' followers in Jerusalem?' they asked. 'And didn't he come here to arrest them and take them in chains to the leading priests?' Saul's preaching became more and more powerful, and the Jews in Damascus couldn't refute his proofs that Jesus was indeed the Messiah. After a while some of the Jews plotted together to kill him. They were watching for him day and night at the city gate so they could murder him, but Saul was told about their plot. So during the night, some of the other believers lowered him in a large basket through an opening in the city wall. When Saul arrived in Jerusalem, he tried to meet with the believers, but they were all afraid of him. They did not believe he had truly become a believer! Then Barnabas brought him to the apostles and told them how Saul had seen the Lord on the way to Damascus and how the Lord had spoken to Saul. He also told them that Saul had preached boldly in the name of Jesus in Damascus. So Saul stayed with the apostles and went all around Jerusalem with them, preaching boldly in the name of the Lord."

The first time we see the name Saul being used synonymously with the name of Paul is in Acts 13:9–10 where it says, "Saul, also known as Paul, was filled with the Holy Spirit, and he looked the sorcerer in the eye. Then he said, 'You son of the devil, full of every sort of deceit and fraud, and enemy of all that is good! Will you never stop perverting the true ways of the Lord?'" As the saying goes, the rest is history. Paul goes on to become one of the most important and influential characters in the Bible. He is proof, that no matter our past, any one of us can be used by the Lord. Paul represents how the power of Christ can convert even the most revolting nonbeliever, into a believer who can do so much to further the Kingdom of God.

Do you have reservations in believing Jesus actually existed and was the Son of God? There's a reason why Paul's story is documented and has survived the test of time. Paul is that beacon of Light that shows the world, Christ not only lived then, but He lives today. If you are a follower of Christ, do you have thoughts that you are not worthy to be used by God? Do you wonder if God would ever use you? The Good News is He can, and He will. We need to look for the opportunities that God provides, for us to witness for Christ. We need to take on the responsibility of helping others find Christ. We can make a difference, but the difference starts with each of us. We must first be willing to change ourselves before we can expect to affect change in others.

Paul lived during a time when the New Testament was his reality. We live during a time when the New Testament is our history. No matter where you are in your personal relationship with Christ, no matter the intensity of your Light, you need to nurture your relationship, so your Light can become brighter. Paul started about as dark as you can get, and yet, he became one of the brightest beacons of Light. That Light continues to shine bright to this day.

What makes you think you are different than any of the characters in the Bible? Why would you think you're not worthy? Why would you think it can't be you? No matter where you are in your spiritual walk, you need to keep striving to be the best you can be, in Christ. You need to shine your Light to become that beacon of hope for others. Paul says in Second Corinthians 5:17–20, "This means that anyone who belongs to Christ has become a new person. The old life is gone; a new life has begun! And all of this is a gift from God, who brought us back to himself through Christ. And God has given us this task of reconciling people to him. For God was in Christ, reconciling the world to himself, no longer counting people's sins against them. And he gave us the wonderful message of reconciliation. So we are Christ's ambassadors; God is making his appeal through us. We speak for Christ when we plead, 'Come back to God!'" If we don't embrace this task of reconciling people to God, who will? Don't miss your opportunity to be an ambassador for Christ.

About the Author

Bruce is a biblical counselor by degree. But he believes that no matter how much someone is biblically counseled, without the personal awareness and dependence on the Spirit of God, there won't be a change of heart, and there won't be a long-lasting change of behavior. We are all spiritually transforming. We are all discovering who God is and His plans for us. But we must not only listen to God, we must be willing to obey Him. Because Bruce listened and obeyed, he was inspired to write *Battle Cry*.

Bruce's call into ministry is unique. After graduating from high school at the young age of seventeen, he enlisted in the navy and served his country as a medic. After serving in the military, he attended college and worked for the postal service part time. Thirty-four years later, at the age of fifty-seven, he retired as a postmaster. Several months before retiring, while sitting on his back porch reading his Bible, Bruce felt the Spirit call him into ministry. He heard the Spirit say, "Your grandfather was a minister, and your son is a minister, do you not see you are a missing link?"

Bruce answered the call by going back to college. He graduated with honors from Trinity College of the Bible and Trinity Theological Seminary with a BA in biblical counseling. He later became an ordained minister, and he and his wife of forty-two years, started a homeless outreach ministry called RV Ambassadors for Christ. While blessed to travel around the country in an RV, wherever they go, they seek those who are homeless. They offer water, soap, deodorant, toothbrush, toothpaste, razor, hand sanitizer, socks, snacks, and a *New Testament Bible*. When possible, they try to meet individual needs by providing specific items such as gloves, coats, shoes, sleeping bags, and bed-rolls. In Matthew 25:40 Jesus says, "And the King will say, 'I tell you the truth, when you did it to one of the least of these my brothers and sisters, you were doing it to me!'"

Bruce's hope and prayer is, as you read *Battle Cry*, you are spiritually inspired and motivated to pursue a personal and more meaningful relationship with Christ. Bruce believes your relationship with Christ is directly tied to your spiritual strength. Through the strength of the Spirit, and by following the Spirit's lead, you will discover all that God has planned for you.

Visit Bruce online at:

brucedillender.com
battlecrythebook.com
battlecrygoodvsevil.com